MILLIONAIRE MIND COURSE CERTIFICATE

T. Harv Eker and Peak Potentials Training invite you and one family member to attend the Millionaire Mind Intensive Seminar, as complimentary guests. To register and for more information go to **www.millionairemindbook.com.**

If you have no access to a computer, call toll-free **1-888-6BeRich.***

Use Reference #_____
when you register.

(If you were not given a Reference #, use your book receipt # or special promotion code.)

---

* The offer is open to all purchasers of *Secrets of the Millionaire Mind* by T. Harv Eker. Original proof of purchase is required. The offer is limited to the Millionaire Mind Intensive weekend seminar only, and your registration in the seminar is subject to availability of space and/or changes to program schedule. This is a limited time offer and the course must be completed by the date shown on the website www.millionairemind.com. The value of this free admission for you and a companion is $2,590, as of February 2005. There will be an administration fee or deposit taken upon registration. Corporate or organizational purchasers may not use one book to invite more than two people. While participants will be responsible for their travel and other costs, admission to the program is complimentary. Participants in the seminars are under no additional financial obligation whatsoever to Peak Potentials Training or T. Harv Eker. Peak Potentials Training reserves the right to refuse admission to anyone it believes may disrupt the seminar, and to remove from the premises anyone it believes is disrupting the seminar.

w/ ♡

Secrets of the **Millionaire Mind**

Mastering the Inner Game of Wealth

T. Harv Eker

Collins
An Imprint of HarperCollinsPublishers

The offer on page 193 is open to all purchasers of *Secrets of the Millionaire Mind* by T. Harv Eker. Original proof of purchase is required. The offer is limited to the Millionaire Mind Intensive weekend seminar only, and your registration in the seminar is subject to availability of space and/or changes to program schedule. This is a limited time offer and the course must be completed by the date shown on the website www.millionairemindbook.com. The value of this free admission for you and a companion is $2,590, as of February 2005. There will be an administration fee or deposit. Corporate or organizational purchasers may not use one book to invite more than two people. While participants will be responsible for their travel and other costs, admission to the program is complimentary. Participants in the seminars are under no additional financial obligation whatsoever to Peak Potentials Training or T. Harv Eker. Peak Potentials Training reserves the right to refuse admission to anyone it believes may disrupt the seminar, and to remove from the premises anyone it believes is disrupting the seminar.

This book is not intended to provide personalized legal, accounting, financial, or investment advice. Readers are encouraged to seek the counsel of competent professionals with regard to such matters as interpretation of the law, proper accounting procedures, financial planning, and investment strategies. The Author and Publisher specifically disclaim any liability, loss, or risk which is incurred as a consequence, directly or indirectly, of the use and application of any of the contents of this work.

HarperCollins books may be purchased for educational, business, or sales promotional use. For information, please write: Special Markets Department, HarperCollins Publishers Inc., 10 East 53rd Street, New York, NY 10022.

FIRST EDITION

Designed by RLF Design

Library of Congress Cataloging-in-Publication Data
Eker, T. Harv
  Secrets of the millionaire mind: mastering the inner game of wealth/T. Harv Eker.
    p. cm.
  Includes index.
  ISBN 0-06-076328-0
  1. Money—Psychological aspects. 2. Millionaires—Psychology.
3. Rich people—Psychology. 4. Wealth—Psychological aspects.
5. Capitalists and financiers—Psychology. 6. Success in business—
Psychological aspects. I. Title.

HG222.3.E37 2005
332.024'01—dc22   2004054344

    07 08 09 DIX/RRD 50 49 48 47 46 45 44 43

More Praise for T. Harv Eker and *Secrets of the Millionaire Mind*

"T. Harv Eker gives us a blueprint and the tools to build our house of wealth, from the inside out, so it will stand the test of time and circumstance."

—Dr. Denis Waitley, author, *Seeds of Greatness*

"T. Harv Eker is a master at making the road to riches simple. Finally, his powerful principles are available in this amazing book."

—Marci Shimoff, coauthor, *Chicken Soup for the Woman's Soul*

"Study this book as if your life depended on it . . . financially it may!"

—Anthony Robbins, the world's #1 peak performance coach

"*Secrets of the Millionaire Mind* is *the* bible for creating wealth in a practical way. T. Harv Eker dispels the myths and makes millionaire secrets accessible to every person. Devour this book!"

—Jill Lublin, best-selling author,
Networking Magic and *Guerrilla Publicity*

"Harv Eker is one of the most extraordinary trainers in the world today! Harv's experiential techniques are transformational, and he creates amazing results every time he speaks!"

—Mark Victor Hansen, cocreator,
Chicken Soup for the Soul®, more than 70 million sold;
coauthor, *The One Minute Millionaire*

ACKNOWLEDGMENTS

Writing a book appears to be an individual project, but the reality is that if you want it to be read by thousands or hopefully millions of people, it takes an entire team. I'd first like to thank my wife, Rochelle, my daughter, Madison, and my son, Jesse. Thank you for allowing me the space to do what I came here to do. I'd also like to thank my parents, Sam and Sara, as well as my sister, Mary, and brother-in-law, Harvey, for your unending love and support. Next, a huge thank you to Gail Balsillie, Michelle Burr, Shelley Wenaus, Robert Riopel, Donna Fox, and the entire team at Peak Potentials Training for all your hard work and dedication to making a positive contribution to people's lives as well as making Peak Potentials one of the fastest growing personal development companies in the world.

Thank you to my brilliant book agent, Bonnie Solow, for your ongoing assistance, encouragement, and for leading me through the ins and outs of the book business. Another big thank-you goes to the team at HarperBusiness: publisher Steve Hanselman, who had the vision for this project and put so much time and energy into it; my wonderful editor, Herb Schaffner; marketing director Keith Pfeffer; and publicity director Larry Hughes. A special thanks goes to my colleagues Jack Canfield, Robert G. Allen, and Mark Victor Hansen for your friendship and continued support from the beginning.

Finally, I am deeply grateful to all of the Peak Potentials seminar attendees, support staff, and joint venture partners. Without you, there would be no life-changing seminars.

CONTENTS

"Who the Heck Is T. Harv Eker, and Why Should I Read This Book?"

PEOPLE ARE SHOCKED, AT THE BEGINNING OF MY seminars, when one of the first things I tell them is "Don't believe a word I say." Why would I suggest that? Because I can only speak from my own experience. None of the concepts and insights I share are inherently true or false, right or wrong. They simply reflect my own results, and the amazing results I've seen in the lives of thousands and thousands of my students. Having said that, however, I believe that if you use the principles you learn in this book, you will totally transform your life. Don't just read this book. Study it as if your life depended on it. Then try the principles out for yourself. Whatever works, keep doing. Whatever doesn't, you're welcome to throw away.

I know I may be biased, but when it comes to money, this may be the most important book you have ever read. I understand that's a bold statement, but the fact is, this book provides the missing link between your desire for success and your achievement of success. As you've probably found out by now, those are two different worlds.

No doubt you've read other books, listened to tapes or CDs, gone to courses, and learned about numerous get-rich systems be they in real estate, stocks, or business. But what happened? For most people, not much! They get a short blast of energy, and then it's back to the status quo.

Finally, there's an answer. It's simple, it's law, and you're not going to circumvent it. It all comes down to this: if your subconscious "financial blueprint" is not "set" for success, nothing you learn, nothing you know, and nothing you do will make much of a difference.

In the pages of this book, we will demystify for you why some people are destined to be rich and others are destined for a life of struggle. You will understand the root causes of success, mediocrity, or financial failure and begin changing your financial future for the better. You will understand how childhood influences shape our financial blueprint and how these influences can lead to self-defeating thoughts and habits. You will experience powerful declarations that will help you replace your nonsupportive ways of thinking with mental "wealth files" so that you think—and succeed—just as rich people do. You will also learn practical, step-by-step strategies for increasing your income and building wealth.

In Part I of this book, we will explain how each of us is conditioned to think and act when it comes to money, and outline four key strategies for revising our mental money blueprint. In Part II, we examine the differences between how rich, middle-class, and poor people think, and provide seventeen attitudes and actions to take that will lead to permanent changes in your financial life. Throughout the book we also share just a few examples of the thousands of letters and e-mails I've received from students who have attended the Millionaire Mind Intensive Seminar and achieved powerful results in their lives.

So what is my experience? Where am I coming from? Was I always successful? I wish!

Like many of you, I supposedly had a lot of "potential" but had little to show for it. I read all the books, listened to all the tapes, and went to all the seminars. I really, really, really wanted to be successful. I don't know whether it was for the money, the freedom, the sense of achievement, or just to prove I was good enough in my parents' eyes, but I was almost obsessed with becoming a "success." During my twenties, I started several different businesses, each with the dream of making my fortune, but my results went from dismal to worse.

I worked my butt off but kept coming up short. I had "Loch Ness monster disease": I had heard of this thing called profit, I just never saw any of it. I kept thinking, "If I just get into the right business, get on the right horse, I'll make it." But I was wrong. Nothing was working . . . at least for me. And it was the last part of that sentence that finally struck me. How come others were succeeding in the exact same business I was in and I was still broke? What happened to "Mr. Potential"?

So I began doing some serious soul-searching. I examined my true beliefs and saw that even though I said I really wanted to be rich, I had some deep-rooted worries about it. Mostly I was afraid. Afraid that I might fail, or worse, succeed and then somehow lose it all. Then I'd really be a schmuck. Worse, I would blow the one thing I had going for me: my "story" that I had all this "potential." What if I found out I didn't have what it took and I was destined to a life of struggle?

Then, as luck would have it, I got some advice from an extremely rich friend of my father's. He was at my parents' house playing cards with the "boys" and, in passing, noticed me. This was the third time I'd moved back home, and I was living in the "lower-level suite," otherwise known as the basement. I suppose my dad had complained to him of my woeful existence because when he saw me, he had the sympathy in his eyes usually reserved for the bereaved at a funeral.

He said, "Harv, I started in the same way as you, a complete disaster." Great, I thought, this was making me feel a lot better. I should let him know that I was busy . . . watching the paint peel off the wall.

He kept going: "But then I got some advice that changed my life, and I'd like to pass it on to you." Oh, no, here comes the father-son lecture, and he's not even my father! Finally he came out with it: "Harv, if you're not doing as well as you'd like, all that means is there's something you don't know." Being a brash young man at the time, I thought I knew pretty well everything, but alas, my bank account said something different. So I finally began to listen. He continued, "Did you know that most rich people think in very similar ways?"

I said, "No, I never really considered that." To which he replied, "It's not an exact science, but for the most part, rich people think a certain way and poor people think a completely different way, and those ways of thinking determine their actions and therefore determine their results." He went on, "If you thought the way rich people do and did what rich people do, do you believe you could become rich too?" I remember answering with all the confidence of a mush ball, "I think so." "Then," he replied, "all you have to do is copy how rich people think."

Being the skeptic I was at the time, I said, "So what are you thinking right now?" To which he replied, "I'm thinking that rich people keep their commitments and mine is to your dad right now. The guys are waiting for me, see ya." Although he walked out, what he said sank in.

Nothing else was working in my life, so I figured what the heck and threw myself wholeheartedly into studying rich people and how they think. I learned everything I could about the inner workings of the mind, but concentrated primarily on the psychology of money and success. I discovered that it was true: rich people really *do* think differently from poor and even middle-class people. Eventually, I became aware of how my own thoughts were holding me back from wealth. More important, I learned several powerful techniques and strategies to actually recondition my mind so that I would think in the same ways rich people do.

Finally, I said, "Enough yakking about it, let's put it to the test." I decided to attempt yet another business. Because I was really into health and exercise, I opened one of the first retail fitness stores in North America. I didn't have any money, so I had to borrow $2,000 on my Visa card to get the business started. I began using what I'd learned by modeling rich people, both in terms of their business strategies and their thinking strategies. The first thing I did was commit to my success and playing to win. I swore I would focus and not even consider leaving this business until I was a millionaire or more. This was radically different from my previous efforts, where, because I always thought short-term, I would constantly get sidetracked by either good opportunities or when things got tough.

I also began challenging my mental approach whenever I began thinking in financially negative or counterproductive ways. In the past, I believed that what my mind said was truth. I learned that in many ways, my mind was my biggest obstacle to success. I chose not to entertain thoughts that did not empower me toward my vision of wealth. I used every one of the principles you are going to learn in this book. Did it work? Boy, did it work!

The business was so successful that I opened ten stores in only two and a half years. I then sold half the company shares to a Fortune 500 company for $1.6 million.

After that, I moved to sunny San Diego. I took a couple of years off to refine my strategies and began doing one-on-one business consulting. I presume it was quite effective for people because they kept bringing friends, partners, and associates to our sessions. Soon I was coaching ten and sometimes twenty people at a time.

One of my clients suggested that I might as well open up a school. I thought that was a great idea, so I did. I founded the Street Smart Business School and taught thousands of people all across North America "street-smart" business strategies for "high-speed" success.

As I traveled across the continent giving my seminars, I noticed something strange: You could have two people sitting side by side in exactly the same room, learning exactly the same principles and strategies. One person would take these tools and skyrocket to success. But what do you think might happen to the person sitting right next to him or her? The answer is, not much!

That's when it became obvious that you can have the

greatest "tools" in the world, but if you've got a tiny leak in your "toolbox" (I'm pointing to my head right now), you've got a problem. So I designed a program called the Millionaire Mind Intensive based on the inner game of money and success. When I combined the inner game (the toolbox) with the outer game (the tools), virtually everybody's results went through the roof! So that's what you're going to learn in this book: how to master the inner game of money to win the game of money—how to think rich to get rich!

People often ask me whether my success was a "one-shot deal" or whether it has continued. Let me put it this way: Using the exact principles I teach, I have now earned millions and millions of dollars and am a multimultimillionaire several times over. Virtually all my investments and business ventures seem to skyrocket! Some people tell me I have the "Midas touch," where everything I get involved in turns to gold. They're right, but what they may not realize is that having a Midas touch is simply another way of saying, having a "financial blueprint" set for success, which is exactly what you will have once you learn these principles and do this work.

Early on during our Millionaire Mind Intensive Seminar, I generally ask the audience, "How many of you came here to learn?" It's a bit of a trick question because as author Josh Billings said, "It's not what we don't know that prevents us from succeeding; it's what we know that just ain't so that is our greatest obstacle." This book is not as much about learning as it is about "unlearning"! It is essential you recognize how your old ways of thinking and acting have gotten you exactly where you are right now.

If you're really rich and really happy, fine. But if you're not, I invite you to consider some possibilities that may not fit into your "box" of what you currently think is right or even appropriate for you.

Even though I suggest that you "don't believe a word I say" and want you to test these concepts out in your own life, I'm going to ask you to trust the ideas you are reading. Not because you know me personally, but because thousands and thousands of people have already changed their lives as a result of the principles in this book.

Speaking of trust, it reminds me of one of my favorite stories. It's about a man who is walking along a cliff and all of a sudden loses his balance, slips, and falls off. Fortunately, he has the presence of mind to grab on to the ledge, and he's hanging there for dear life. He hangs and hangs and finally yells out, "Is there anybody up there who can help me?" There's no answer. He keeps calling and calling, "Is there anybody up there who can help me?" Finally this big bellowing voice calls back, "This is God. I can help you. Just let go and trust." Next thing you hear: "Is there anybody *else* up there who can help me?"

The lesson is simple. If you want to move to a higher level of life, you have to be willing to let go of some of your old ways of thinking and being and adopt new ones. The results will eventually speak for themselves.

PART ONE

Your Money Blueprint

WE LIVE IN A WORLD OF DUALITY: UP AND DOWN, light and dark, hot and cold, in and out, fast and slow, right and left. These are but a few examples of the thousands of opposite poles. For one pole to exist, the other pole must also exist. Is it possible to have a right side without a left side? Not a chance.

Consequently, just as there are "outer" laws of money, there must be "inner" laws. The outer laws include things like business knowledge, money management, and investment strategies. These are essential. But the inner game is just as important. An analogy would be a carpenter and his tools. Having top-of-the-line tools is imperative, but being the top-notch carpenter who masterfully uses those tools is even more critical.

I have a saying: "It's not enough to be in the right place at the right time. You have to be the right *person* in the right place at the right time."

So who are you? How do you think? What are your beliefs? What are your habits and traits? How do you really feel about yourself? How confident are you in yourself? How well do you relate to others? How much do you trust others?

Do you truly feel that you deserve wealth? What is your ability to act in spite of fear, in spite of worry, in spite of inconvenience, in spite of discomfort? Can you act when you're not in the mood?

The fact is that your character, your thinking, and your beliefs are a critical part of what determines the level of your success.

One of my favorite authors, Stuart Wilde, puts it this way: "The key to success is to raise your own energy; when you do, people will naturally be attracted to you. And when they show up, bill 'em!"

WEALTH PRINCIPLE:
Your income can grow only to the extent you do!

Why Is Your Money Blueprint Important?

Have you heard of people who have "blown up" financially? Have you noticed how some people have a lot of money and then lose it, or have excellent opportunities start well but then go sour on them? Now you know the real cause. On the outside it looks like bad luck, a downturn in the economy, a lousy partner, whatever. On the inside, however, it's another matter. That's why, if you come into big money when you're not ready for it on the inside, the chances are your wealth will be short-lived and you will lose it.

The vast majority of people simply do not have the internal capacity to create and hold on to large amounts of money and the increased challenges that go with more money and success. That, my friends, is the primary reason they don't have much money.

A perfect example is lottery winners. Research has shown again and again that regardless of the size of their winnings, most lottery winners eventually return to their original financial state, the amount they can comfortably handle.

On the other hand, the opposite occurs for self-made millionaires. Notice that when self-made millionaires lose their money, they usually have it back within a relatively short time. Donald Trump is a good example. Trump was worth billions, lost everything, and then a couple of years later, got it all back again and more.

Why does this phenomenon occur? Because even though some self-made millionaires may lose their money, they never lose the most important ingredient to their success: their millionaire mind. Of course in "The Donald"'s case, it's his "billionaire" mind. Do you realize Donald Trump could never be *just* a millionaire? If Donald Trump had a net worth of only 1 million dollars, how do you think he'd feel about his financial success? Most people would agree that he'd probably feel broke, like a financial failure!

That's because Donald Trump's financial "thermostat" is set for billions, not millions. Most people's financial thermostats are set for generating thousands, not millions of dollars; some people's financial thermostats are set for generating hundreds, not even thousands; and some people's financial thermostats are set for below zero. They're frickin' freezing and they don't have a clue as to why!

The reality is that most people do not reach their full potential. Most people are not successful. Research shows that 80 percent of individuals will never be financially free in the way they'd like to be, and 80 percent will never claim to be truly happy.

The reason is simple. Most people are unconscious. They are a little asleep at the wheel. They work and think on a superficial level of life—based only on what they can see. They live strictly in the visible world.

The Roots Create the Fruits

Imagine a tree. Let's suppose this tree represents the tree of life. On this tree there are fruits. In life, our fruits are called our results. So we look at the fruits (our results) and we don't like them; there aren't enough of them, they're too small, or they don't taste good.

So what do we tend to do? Most of us put even more attention and focus on the fruits, our results. But what is it that actually creates those particular fruits? It's the seeds and the roots that create those fruits.

It's what's *under the ground* that creates what's above the ground. It's what's *invisible* that creates what's *visible*. So what does that mean? It means that if you want to change the fruits, you will first have to change the roots. If you want to change the visible, you must first change the invisible.

WEALTH PRINCIPLE:
If you want to change the fruits, you will first have to change the roots. If you want to change the visible, you must first change the invisible.

Of course, some say that seeing is believing. The question I have for such people is "Why do you bother paying your electric bill?" Although you cannot see electricity, you can certainly recognize and use its power. If you have any doubt as to whether it exists, just stick your finger in an electric socket, and I guarantee that your doubts will quickly disappear.

In my experience, what you cannot see in this world is far more powerful than anything you can see. You may or may not agree with this statement, but to the extent that you do not apply this principle in your life, you must be suffering. Why? Because you are going against the laws of nature, whereby what is under the ground creates what is above the ground, where what is invisible creates what is visible.

As humans, we are a part of nature, not above it. Consequently, when we align with the laws of nature and work on our roots—our "inner" world—our life flows smoothly. When we don't, life gets rough.

In every forest, on every farm, in every orchard on earth, it's what's under the ground that creates what's above the ground. That's why placing your attention on the fruits that you have already grown is futile. You cannot change the fruits that are already hanging on the tree. You can, however, change tomorrow's fruits. But to do so, you will have to dig below the ground and strengthen the roots.

The Four Quadrants

One of the most important things you can ever understand is that we do not live on only one plane of existence. We live in at least four different realms at once. These four quadrants are the physical world, the mental world, the emotional world, and the spiritual world.

What most people never realize is that the physical realm is merely a "printout" of the other three.

For example, let's suppose you've just written a letter on your computer. You hit the print key and the letter comes out of your printer. You look at your hard copy, and lo and behold, you find a typo. So you take out your trusty eraser and rub out the typo. Then you hit print again and out comes the same typo.

Oh my gosh, how could this be? You just erased it! So this time you get a bigger eraser and you rub even harder and longer. You even study a three-hundred-page manual called *Effective Erasing*. Now you've got all the "tools" and knowledge you need. You're ready. You hit print and there it is again! "No way!" you cry out, stunned in amazement. "How could this be? What's going on here? Am I in the twilight zone?"

What's going on here is that the real problem cannot be changed in the "printout," the physical world; it can only be changed in the "program," the mental, emotional, and spiritual worlds.

Money is a result, wealth is a result, health is a result, illness is a result, your weight is a result. We live in a world of cause and effect.

WEALTH PRINCIPLE:
Money is a result, wealth is a result, health is a
result, illness is a result, your weight is a result.
We live in a world of cause and effect.

Have you ever heard someone assert that a lack of money was a bit of a problem? Now hear this: A lack of money is never, ever, ever a problem. A lack of money is merely a symptom of what is going on underneath.

Lack of money is the effect, but what is the root cause? It boils down to this. The only way to change your "outer" world is to first change your "inner" world.

Whatever results you're getting, be they rich or poor, good or bad, positive or negative, always remember that your outer world is simply a reflection of your inner world. If things aren't going well in your outer life, it's because things aren't going well in your inner life. It's that simple.

Declarations: A Powerful Secret for Change

In my seminars we use "accelerated learning" techniques that allow you to learn faster and remember more of what you learn. The key is "involvement." Our approach follows from the old saying "What you hear, you forget; what you see, you remember; what you do, you understand."

So I'm going to ask that every time you reach the end of a major principle in this book, you first put your hand on your heart, then make a verbal "declaration," then touch your head with your index finger and make another verbal "declaration." What's a declaration? It's simply a positive statement that you make emphatically, out loud.

Why are declarations such a valuable tool? Because everything is made of one thing: energy. All energy travels in frequencies and vibrations. Therefore, each declaration you make carries its own vibrational frequency. When you state a declaration aloud, its energy vibrates throughout the cells of your body, and by touching your body at the same time, you can feel its unique resonance. Declarations not only send a specific message to the universe, they also send a powerful message to your subconscious mind.

The difference between a declaration and an affirmation is slight, but in my mind, powerful. The definition of an affirmation is "a positive statement asserting that a goal you wish to achieve is already happening." The definition of a declaration is "to state an official intention to undertake a particular course of action or adopt a particular status."

An affirmation states that a goal is already happening. I'm not crazy about this because, often when we affirm something that is not yet real, the little voice in our head usually responds with "This isn't true, this is BS."

On the other hand, a declaration is not saying something is true, it's stating that we have an intention of doing or being something. This is a position the little voice can buy, because we're not stating it's true right now, but again, it's an intention for us in the future.

A declaration, by definition, is also *official.* It is a formal statement of energy into the universe and throughout your body.

Another word from the definition is important—*action.* You must take all the actions necessary to make your intention a reality.

I recommend that you state your declarations aloud each morning and each evening. Doing your declarations while looking into a mirror will accelerate the process even more.

Now I have to admit that when I first heard of all this, I said, "No way. This declaration stuff is far too hokey for me." But because I was broke at the time, I decided, "What the heck, it can't hurt," and started doing them. Now I'm rich, so it shouldn't come as a big surprise that I believe that declarations really work.

Either way, I'd rather be really hokey and really rich than really cool and really broke. How about you?

That said, I invite you to place your hand on your heart and repeat the following . . .

DECLARATION:

"My inner world creates my outer world."

Now touch your head and say . . .

"I have a millionaire mind."

As a special bonus, if you go to **www.millionairemind book.com** and click on "FREE BOOK BONUSES," we will give you a free list of all the declarations in this book presented in calligraphy, in a printable format, suitable for framing.

What Is Your Money Blueprint and How Is It Formed?

Whether I'm appearing on radio or television, I'm well-known for making the following statement: "Give me five minutes, and I can predict your financial future for the rest of your life."

WEALTH PRINCIPLE:
Give me five minutes, and I can predict your
financial future for the rest of your life.

How? In a short conversation, I can identify what's called your money and success "blueprint." Each of us has a personal money and success blueprint already embedded in our subconscious mind. And this blueprint, more than anything and everything else combined, will determine your financial destiny.

What is a money blueprint? As an analogy, let's consider the blueprint for a house, which is a preset plan or design for that particular home. In the same way, your money blueprint is simply your preset program or way of being in relation to money.

I want to introduce you to an extremely important formula. It determines how you create your reality and wealth. Many of the most respected teachers in the field of human potential have used this formula as a foundation for their teachings. Called the Process of Manifestation, it goes like this:

$$T \to F \to A = R$$

WEALTH PRINCIPLE:
Thoughts lead to feelings.
Feelings lead to actions.
Actions lead to results.

Your financial blueprint consists of a combination of your thoughts, feelings, and actions in the arena of money.

So how is your money blueprint formed? The answer is simple. Your financial blueprint consists primarily of the information or "programming" you received in the past, and especially as a young child.

Who were the primary sources of this programming or conditioning? For most people, the list includes parents, siblings, friends, authority figures, teachers, religious leaders, media, and your culture, to name a few.

Let's take culture. Isn't it true that certain cultures have one way of thinking and dealing with money, while other cultures have a different approach? Do you think a child comes out of the womb with his or her attitudes toward money, or do you believe the child is *taught* how to deal with money? That's right. Every child is taught how to think about and act in relation to money.

The same holds true for you, for me, for everyone. You were taught how to think and act when it comes to money. These teachings become your conditioning, which becomes automatic responses that run you for the rest of your life. Unless, of course, you intercede and revise your mind's money files. This is exactly what we are going to do in this book, and what we do for thousands of people each year, on a deeper and more permanent level at the Millionaire Mind Intensive Seminar.

We said earlier that thoughts lead to feelings, that feelings lead to actions, that actions lead to results. So here's an interesting question: Where do your thoughts come from? Why do you think differently from the next person?

Your thoughts originate from the "files of information" you have in the storage cabinets of your mind. So where does this information come from? It comes from your past programming. That's right, your past conditioning determines every thought that bubbles up in your mind. That's why it's often referred to as the conditioned mind.

To reflect this understanding, we can now revise our Process of Manifestation in the following manner:

$$P \rightarrow T \rightarrow F \rightarrow A = R$$

Your programming leads to your thoughts; your thoughts lead to your feelings; your feelings lead to your actions; your actions lead to your results.

Therefore, just as is done with a personal computer, by changing your programming, you take the first essential step to changing your results.

So how are we conditioned? We are conditioned in three primary ways in every arena of life, including money:

Verbal programming: What did you *hear* when you were young?

Modeling: What did you *see* when you were young?

Specific incidents: What did you *experience* when you were young?

The three aspects of conditioning are important to understand, so let's go over each of them. In Part II of this book, you will learn how to recondition yourself for wealth and success.

The First Influence: Verbal Programming

Let's begin with *verbal* programming. What did you hear about money, wealth, and rich people when you were growing up?

Did you ever hear phrases like *money is the root of all evil, save your money for a rainy day, rich people are greedy, rich people are criminals, filthy rich, you have to work hard to make money, money doesn't grow on trees, you can't be rich and spiritual, money doesn't buy happiness, money talks, the rich get richer and the poor get poorer, that's not for people like us, not everyone can be rich, there's never enough,* and the infamous *we can't afford it?*

In my household, every time I asked my father for any money I'd hear him scream, "What am I made of . . . money?" Jokingly I'd respond, "I wish. I'll take an arm, a hand, even a finger." He never laughed once.

Here's the rub. All the statements you heard about money when you were young remain in your subconscious mind as part of the blueprint that is running your financial life.

Verbal conditioning is extremely powerful. For example, when my son, Jesse, was three years old, he ran over to me and excitedly said, "Daddy, let's go see the Ninja Turtle movie. It's playing near us." For the life of me, I couldn't figure out how this toddler could already be a master of geography. A couple of hours later, I got my answer in the form of a TV commercial advertising the movie, which had at the end the usual tagline: "Now playing at a theater near you."

Another example of the power of verbal conditioning came at the expense of one of our Millionaire Mind seminar participants. Stephen didn't have a problem *earning* money; his challenge was *keeping* it.

At the time Stephen came to the course he was earning over $800,000 a year and had been doing so for the past nine years. Yet he was still barely scraping by. Somehow, he managed to spend his money, lend it, or lose it all by making poor investment decisions. Whatever the reason, his net worth was exactly zero!

Stephen shared with us that when he was growing up, his mom always used to say, "Rich people are greedy. They make their money off the sweat of the poor. You should have just enough to get by. After that you're a pig."

It doesn't take a rocket scientist to figure out what was going on inside Stephen's subconscious mind. No wonder he was broke. He was verbally conditioned by his mother to believe that rich people are greedy. Therefore, his mind linked up rich with greedy, which of course is *bad*. Since he didn't want to be bad, subconsciously he couldn't be rich.

Stephen loved his mom and didn't want her to disapprove of him. Obviously, based on her beliefs, if he were to get rich, she wouldn't approve. Therefore, the only thing for him to do was to get rid of any extra money beyond just getting by, otherwise he'd be a pig!

Now, you would think that in choosing between being rich and being approved of by Mom or anyone else for that matter, most people would take being rich. Not a chance! The mind just doesn't work that way. Sure, riches would seem to be the logical choice. *But when the subconscious mind must choose between deeply rooted emotions and logic, emotions will almost always win.*

WEALTH PRINCIPLE:
When the subconscious mind must choose
between deeply rooted emotions and logic,
emotions will almost always win.

Let's get back to our story. In less than ten minutes at the course, using some extremely effective experiential techniques, Stephen's money blueprint changed dramatically. In only two years, he went from being broke to becoming a millionaire.

At the course, Stephen began to understand that these nonsupportive beliefs were his mom's, based on her past programming, and not his. We then took it a step further and helped him to create a strategy whereby he wouldn't lose his mother's approval if he got rich. It was simple.

His mom loved Hawaii. So Stephen invested in a beach-front condo on Maui. He sends her there for the entire winter. She's in heaven, and so is he. First, she now loves that he's rich and tells everyone how generous he is. Second, he doesn't have to deal with her for six months of the year. Brilliant!

In my own life, after a slow start, I began doing well in business but never seemed to make money with my stocks. In becoming aware of my money blueprint, I recalled that when I was young, each day after work, my dad would sit down at the dinner table with the newspaper, check the stock pages, slam his fist on the table, and shout, "Those stinkin' stocks!" He then spent the next half hour ranting about how stupid the whole system is and how you have a better chance of making money playing the slot machines in Las Vegas.

Now that you understand the power of verbal conditioning, can you see that it's no wonder I couldn't make any money in the stock market? I was literally programmed to fail, programmed to unconsciously pick the wrong stock, at the wrong price, at the wrong time. Why? To subconsciously validate my money blueprint that said, "Stocks stink!"

All I can say is, by digging out this massive, toxic weed from my inner "financial garden," I began getting inundated with more fruits! Virtually the day after I reconditioned myself, the stocks I chose began to boom, and I've continued to have amazing success in the stock market ever since. It seems incredibly strange, but when you really understand how the money blueprint works, it makes perfect sense.

Again, your subconscious conditioning determines your thinking. Your thinking determines your decisions, and your decisions determine your actions, which eventually determine your outcomes.

There are four key elements of change, each of which is essential in reprogramming your financial blueprint. They are simple but profoundly powerful.

The first element of change is *awareness*. You can't change something unless you know it exists.

The second element of change is *understanding*. By understanding where your "way of thinking" originates, you can recognize that it has to come from outside you.

The third element of change is *disassociation*. Once you realize this way of thinking isn't you, you can separate yourself from it and choose in the present whether to keep it or let it go—based on who you are today, and where you want to be tomorrow. You can observe this way of thinking and see it for what it is, a "file" of information that was stored in your mind a long, long time ago and may not hold any truth or value for you anymore.

The fourth element of change is *reconditioning*. We will begin this process in Part II of this book, where we will introduce you to the mental files that generate wealth. Should you want to take this a step further, I invite you to attend the Millionaire Mind Intensive Seminar, where you will be led through a series of powerful experiential techniques that will rewire your subconscious on a cellular and permanent level—retraining your mind to respond supportively in terms of money and success.

The elements of frequency and ongoing support are also important for lasting change to occur, so I've got another gift to help you. If you go to **www.millionairemindbook .com** and click on "FREE BOOK BONUSES," you can subscribe to the Millionaire Mind "thought of the week." Every seven days you will receive a profound lesson that can assist your success.

Meanwhile, let's go back to our discussion on verbal conditioning and the steps you can take now to begin revising your money blueprint.

Steps for Change: Verbal Programming

AWARENESS: Write down all the statements you heard about money, wealth, and rich people when you were young.

UNDERSTANDING: Write down how you believe these statements have affected your financial life so far.

DISASSOCIATION: Can you see that these thoughts represent only what you learned and are not part of your anatomy and not who you are? Can you see that you have a choice in the present moment to be different?

DECLARATION: Place your hand over your heart and say . . .

"What I heard about money isn't necessarily true. I choose to adopt new ways of thinking that support my happiness and success."

Touch your head and say . . .

"I have a millionaire mind."

The Second Influence: Modeling

The second way we are conditioned is called modeling. What were your parents or guardians like in the arena of money when you were growing up? Did one or both of them manage their money well or did they mismanage it? Were they spenders or savers? Were they shrewd investors or were they noninvestors? Were they risk takers or conservative?

Was money consistently there or was the flow more sporadic? Did money come easily in your family, or was it always a struggle? Was money a source of joy in your household or the cause of bitter arguments?

Why is this information important? You've probably heard the saying "Monkey see, monkey do." Well, humans aren't far behind. As kids, we learn just about everything from modeling.

Although most of us would hate to admit it, there's more than a grain of truth in the old saying "The apple doesn't fall too far from the tree."

This reminds me of the story about a woman who prepares a ham for dinner by cutting off both ends. Her bewildered husband asks why she cuts off the ends. She replies, "That's how my mom cooked it." Well, it just so happened that her mom was coming for dinner that night. So they asked her why she cut off the ends of the ham. Mom replies, "That's how my mom cooked it." So they decide to call Grandma on the phone and ask why she cut off the ends of the ham. Her answer? "Because my pan was too small!"

The point is that generally speaking, we tend to be identical to one or a combination of our parents in the arena of money.

For example, my dad was an entrepreneur. He was in the home-building business. He built anywhere from a dozen to a hundred homes per project. Each project took a huge amount of capital investment. My dad would have to put up everything we had and borrow heavily from the bank until the homes were sold and the cash came through. Consequently, at the beginning of each project, we had no money and were in debt up to our eyeballs.

As you can imagine, during this period my dad was not in

the best of moods nor was generosity his strong suit. If I asked him for anything that cost even a penny, his standard reply after the usual "What am I, made of money?" was "Are you crazy?" Of course, I wouldn't get a dime, but what I would get was that "Don't even think of asking again" glare. I'm sure you know the one.

This scenario would last for about a year or two until the homes were finally sold. Then, we'd be rolling in dough. All of a sudden, my dad was a different person. He'd be happy, kind, and extremely generous. He'd come over and ask me if I needed a few bucks. I felt like giving him his glare back, but I wasn't that stupid so I just said, "Sure, Dad, thanks," and rolled my eyes.

Life was good . . . until that dreaded day when he'd come home and announce, "I found a good piece of land. We're going to build again." I distinctly remember saying, "Great, Dad, good luck," as my heart sank, knowing the struggle that was about to unfold again.

This pattern lasted from the time I could remember, when I was about six, until the age of twenty-one, when I moved out of my parents' house for good. Then it stopped, or so I thought.

At twenty-one years of age, I finished school and became, you guessed it, a builder. I then went on to several other types of project-based businesses. For some strange reason, I'd make a small fortune, but just a short time later, I'd be broke. I'd get into another business and believe I was on top of the world again, only to hit bottom a year later.

This up-and-down pattern went on for nearly ten years before I realized that maybe the problem wasn't the type of business I was choosing, the partners I was choosing, the employees I had, the state of the economy, or my decision to take time off and relax when things were going well. I finally recognized that maybe, just maybe, I was unconsciously re-living my dad's up-and-down income pattern.

All I can say is, thank goodness I learned what you're learning in this book and was able to recondition myself out of that "yo-yo" model and into having a consistently grow-ing income. Today, the urge to change when things are going well (and to sabotage myself in the process) still comes up. But now, there's another file in my mind that observes this feeling and says, "Thank you for sharing; now let's get refo-cused and back to work."

Another example comes from one of my seminars in Or-lando, Florida. As usual, people were filing up to the stage, one by one, to get an autograph and say hello or thank you or whatever. I'll never forget one older gentleman because he came up sobbing. He could barely catch his breath and kept wiping his tears with his sleeve. I asked him what was wrong. He said, "I'm sixty-three years old and I've been reading books and going to seminars since they were invented. I've seen every speaker and tried everything they taught. I've tried stocks, real estate, and been in over a dozen different businesses. I went back to university and got an MBA. I've got more knowledge than ten average men, yet I've never made it financially. I'd always get a good start but end up empty-handed, and in all those years I never knew why. I thought I must just be plain old stupid . . . until today.

"Finally, after listening to you and doing the processes, it all makes sense. There's nothing wrong with me. I just had my dad's money blueprint stuck in my head and that's been my nemesis. My dad went through the heart of the Depres-sion era. Every day he would try getting jobs or selling things and come home empty-handed. I wish I would have understood modeling and money patterns forty years ago. What a waste of time, all that learning and knowledge has been." He began to cry even harder.

I replied, "No way is your knowledge a waste of time! It has just been latent, waiting in a 'mind' bank, waiting for the opportunity to come out. Now that you've formulated a 'success blueprint,' everything you've ever learned will become usable and you will skyrocket to success."

For most of us, when we hear the truth, we know it. He started to lighten up and began breathing deeply again. Then a big grin came across his face. He gave me the biggest hug and said, "Thank you, thank you, thank you." Last I heard from him, everything was booming: he has accumulated more wealth in the last eighteen months than in the past eighteen years combined. I love it!

Again, you can have all the knowledge and skills in the world, but if your "blueprint" isn't set for success, you're financially doomed.

We often get seminar participants whose parents were involved in World War II or who lived through the Depression. These people are often in shock when they realize how much their parents' experiences have influenced their beliefs and habits around money. Some spend like crazy because "You could easily lose all your money, so you might as well enjoy it while you can." Others go the opposite route: they hoard their money and "save for a rainy day."

A word of wisdom: Saving for a rainy day might sound like a good idea, but it can create big problems. One of the principles we teach in another of our courses is the power of intention. If you are saving your money for a *rainy* day, what are you going to get? Rainy days! Stop doing that. Instead of saving for a rainy day, focus on saving for a *joyous* day or for the day you win your financial freedom. Then, by virtue of the law of intention, that's exactly what you will get.

Earlier we said that most of us tend to be identical to one or both parents in the arena of money, but there's also the flip side of the coin. Some of us end up being exactly the opposite of one or both parents. Why would that happen? Do the words *anger* and *rebellion* ring a bell? In short, it just depends on how ticked off you were at them.

Unfortunately, as little kids we can't say to our parents, "Mom and Dad, have a seat. I'd like to discuss something with you. I'm not fond of the way you're managing your money or, for that matter, your lives, and therefore, when I become an adult, I'll be doing things quite differently. I hope you understand. Good night now and pleasant dreams."

No, no, no, it doesn't go quite that way. Instead, when our buttons are pushed, we generally freak out and what comes out sounds more like "I hate you. I'll never be like you. When I grow up, I'm gonna be rich. Then I'll get whatever I want whether you like it or not." Then we run to our bedroom, slam the door, and start pounding our pillow or whatever else is at hand, to vent our frustration.

Many people who come from poor families become angry and rebellious about it. Often they either go out and get rich or at least have the motivation to do so. But there's one little hiccup, which is actually a big burp. Whether such people get rich or work their buns off trying to become successful, they are not usually happy. Why? Because the root of their wealth or motivation for money is anger and resentment. Consequently, *money* and *anger* become linked in their minds, and the more money such individuals have or strive for, the angrier they get.

Eventually, the higher self says, "I'm tired of being angry and stressed out. I just want to be peaceful and happy." So they ask the same mind that created the *link* what to do about this situation. To which their mind answers, "If you want to get rid of your anger, you're going to have to get rid of your money." So they do. They subconsciously get rid of their money.

They overspend or make a poor investment decision or get a financially disastrous divorce, or they sabotage their success in some other way. But no matter, because now these folks are happy. Right? Wrong! Things are even worse because now they're not just angry, they're broke and angry. They got rid of the wrong thing!

They got rid of the money instead of the anger, the fruit instead of the root. Meanwhile, the real issue is, and always was, the anger between them and their parents. And until that anger is resolved, they will never be truly happy or peaceful regardless of how much money they have or don't have.

The reason or motivation you have for making money or creating success is vital. If your motivation for acquiring money or success comes from a nonsupportive root such as fear, anger, or the need to "prove" yourself, your money will never bring you happiness.

WEALTH PRINCIPLE:
If your motivation for acquiring money or success comes from a nonsupportive root such as fear, anger, or the need to "prove" yourself, your money will never bring you happiness.

Why? Because you can't solve any of these issues with money. Take fear, for instance. During my seminars I ask the audience, "How many of you would cite fear as your primary motivation for success?" Not many people put up their hand. However, then I ask, "How many of you would cite security as one of your main motivators for success?" Almost everyone puts up his or her hand. But get this—security and fear are both motivated by the *same* thing. Seeking security comes from insecurity, which is based in fear.

So, will more money dissolve the fear? You wish! But the answer is absolutely not. Why? Because money is not the root of the problem; fear is. What's even worse is that fear is not just a problem, it's a habit. Therefore, making more money will only change the kind of fear we have. When we were broke, we were most likely afraid we'd never make it or never have enough. Once we make it, however, our fear usually changes to "What if I lose what I've made?" or "Everyone's going to want what I have" or "I'm going to get creamed in taxes." In short, until we get to the root of this issue and dissolve the fear, no amount of money will help.

Of course, given a choice, most of us would rather worry about having money and losing it than not having money at all, but neither are overly enlightened ways to live.

As with those of us driven by fear, many people are motivated to achieve financial success to prove they are "good enough." We'll cover this challenge in detail in Part II of this book, but for now, just realize that no amount of money can ever make you good enough. Money can't make you something you already are. Again, as with fear, the "always having to prove yourself" issue becomes your habitual way of living. You don't even recognize it's running you. You call yourself a high achiever, a hard driver, determined, and all these traits are fine. The only question is why? What is the root engine that drives all this?

For people who are driven to prove they are good enough, no amount of money can ease the pain of that inner wound that makes everything and everyone in their life "not enough." No amount of money, or anything else for that matter, will ever be enough for people who feel they are not good enough themselves.

Again, it's all about you. Remember, your inner world reflects your outer world. If you believe you are not enough, you will validate that belief and create the reality that you don't have enough. On the other hand, if you believe you are plenty, you will validate that belief and create plenty of abundance. Why? Because "plenty" will be your root, which will then become your natural way of being.

By unlinking your money motivation from anger, fear, and the need to prove yourself, you can install new links for earning your money through *purpose, contribution,* and *joy.* That way, you'll never have to get rid of your money to be happy.

Being a rebel or the opposite of your parents is not always a problem. To the contrary, if you were a rebel (often the case with second-born children) and your folks had poor money habits, it's probably a good thing that you are their opposite. On the other hand, if your parents were successful and you're rebelling against them, you could be in for serious financial difficulties.

Either way, what's important is to recognize how your way of being relates to one or both of your parents in the arena of money.

Steps for Change: Modeling

AWARENESS: Consider the ways of being and habits each of your parents had around money and wealth. Write down how you may be identical or opposite to either of them.

UNDERSTANDING: Write down the effect this modeling has had on your financial life.

DISASSOCIATION: Can you see this way of being is only what you learned and isn't you? Can you see you have a choice in the present moment to be different?

DECLARATION: Place your hand over your heart and say . . .

"What I modeled around money was their way. I choose my way."

Touch your head and say . . .

"I have a millionaire mind!"

The Third Influence: Specific Incidents

The third primary way in which we are conditioned is by specific incidents. What did you experience when you were young around money, wealth, and rich people? These experiences are extremely important because they shape the beliefs—or rather, the illusions—you now live by.

Let me give you an example. A woman who was an operating-room nurse attended the Millionaire Mind Intensive Seminar. Josey had an excellent income, but somehow she always spent all of her money. When we dug a little deeper, she revealed that when she was eleven years old, she remembers being at a Chinese restaurant with her parents and her sister. Her mom and dad were having yet another bitter argument about money. Her dad was standing up, screaming and slamming his fist on the table. She remembers him turning red, then blue, then falling to the floor from a heart attack. She was on the swim team at school and had CPR training, which she administered, but to no avail. Her father died in her arms.

And so, from that day forth, Josey's mind linked money with *pain*. It's no wonder then that as an adult, she subconsciously got rid of all of her money in an effort to get rid of her pain. It's also interesting to note that she became a nurse. Why? Is it possible that she was still trying to save her dad?

At the course, we helped Josey identify her old money blueprint and revise it. Today she's well on her way to becoming financially free. She's also not a nurse anymore. Not that she didn't enjoy her job. It's just that she was in the nursing profession for the wrong reason. She's now a financial planner, still helping people, but this time one-on-one, to understand how their past programming runs every aspect of their financial lives.

Let me give you another example of a specific incident, one that's closer to home. When my wife was eight years old, she would hear the clanging bells of the ice cream truck coming down the street. She would run to her mom and ask for a quarter. Her mom would reply, "Sorry, dear, I don't have any money. Go ask Dad. Dad's got all the money." My wife would then go ask her dad. He'd give her a quarter, she'd go get her ice cream cone, and she was a happy camper.

Week after week, the same incident would repeat itself. So what did my wife learn about money?

First, that men have all the money. So once we got married, what do you think she expected of me? That's right: money. And I'll tell you what, she wasn't asking for quarters anymore! Somehow she'd graduated.

Second, she learned that women don't have money. If her mom (the deity) didn't have money, obviously this is the way she should be. To validate that way of being, she would subconsciously get rid of all her money. She was quite precise about it too. If you gave her $100, she'd spend $100. If you gave her $200, she'd spend $200. If you gave her $500, she'd spend $500, and if you gave her $1,000, she'd spend $1,000. Then she took one of my courses and learned all about the art of leverage. I gave her $2,000, she spent $10,000! I tried to explain, "No, honey, leverage means we're the ones who are supposed to *get* the ten thousand dollars, not spend it." Somehow it just wasn't sinking in.

The only thing we ever fought about was money. It almost cost us our marriage. What we didn't know at the time was that the meanings each of us attributed to money were radically different. To my wife, money meant immediate *pleasure* (as in enjoying her ice cream). I, on the other hand, grew up with the belief that money was meant to be accumulated as the means to create *freedom.*

As far as I was concerned, whenever my wife spent money, she wasn't spending money, she was spending our future freedom. And as far as she was concerned, whenever I held her back from spending, I was taking away her pleasure in life.

Thank goodness we learned how to revise each of our money blueprints and, more importantly, create a third money blueprint specifically for the relationship.

Success Story from Deborah Chamitoff

From: Deborah Chamitoff
To: T. Harv Eker
Subject: Financially free!

Harv,

Today, I have 18 sources of passive income and I no longer need a J.O.B. Yes, I am rich, but more importantly, my *life* is enriched, joyful, and abundant! But it wasn't always this way.

Money used to be a burden to me. I trusted strangers to manage my financial affairs just so I wouldn't have to deal with it. I lost almost everything during the last stock market crash, and I didn't even realize it until it was too late.

More importantly, I lost my self-respect. Paralyzed with fear, shame, and hopelessness, I withdrew from everyone and everything around me. I continued to punish myself right up until I was dragged to the Millionaire Mind.

During that transformational weekend, I reclaimed my power and resolved to take control of my own financial destiny. I embraced the Declarations of Wealth and forgave myself for past mistakes, truly believing that I deserved to be wealthy.

And now, I'm actually having fun managing my own money! I am financially free and know I always will be because I have a Millionaire Mind!

Thank you, Harv . . . thank you.

Does all this work? Let me put it this way; I've witnessed three miracles in my life:

1. The birth of my daughter.
2. The birth of my son.
3. My wife and I not fighting about money anymore!

Statistics show that the number one cause of all relationship breakups is money. The biggest reason behind the fights people have about money is not the money itself, but the mismatch of their "blueprints." It doesn't matter how much money you have or don't have. If your blueprint doesn't match that of the person you're dealing with, you'll have a major challenge. This goes for married couples, dating couples, family relationships, and even business associates. The key is to comprehend that you are dealing with blueprints, not money. Once you recognize a person's money blueprint, you can deal with your partner in a way that works for both of you. You can begin by becoming aware that your partner's money files are probably not the same as yours. Instead of getting upset, choose understanding. Do your best to find out what's important to your partner in the arena of money and identify his or her motivations and fears. In this way, you'll be dealing with the roots instead of the fruits and have a good shot of making it work. Otherwise, no way, Jose!

One of the most important things you will learn, should you decide to attend the Millionaire Mind Intensive Seminar, is how to recognize your partner's money blueprint as well as how to create a brand-new blueprint between both of you that helps you as partners get what you really want. It is truly a blessing to be able to do this, as it alleviates one of the biggest causes of pain for most people.

Steps for Change: Specific Incidents

Here's an exercise you can do with your partner. Sit down and discuss the history each of you brings to your thoughts about money—what you heard when you were young, what was modeled in your family, and any emotional incidents that occurred. Also, find out what money really means to your partner. Is it pleasure or freedom or security or status? This will assist you in identifying each other's current money blueprint and may help you discover why you might be disagreeing in this arena.

Next, discuss what you want today not as individuals, but as a partnership. Decide and agree upon your general goals and attitudes with regard to money and success. Then create a list of these attitudes and actions you both agree to live by and write them down. Post them on the wall, and if ever there's an issue, gently, very gently, remind each other what you decided together when you were both objective, unemotional, and outside the grip of your old money blueprints.

> **AWARENESS:** Consider a specific emotional incident you experienced around money when you were young.
>
> **UNDERSTANDING:** Write down how this incident may have affected your current financial life.
>
> **DISASSOCIATION:** Can you see this way of being is only what you learned and isn't you? Can you see you have a choice in the present moment to be different?
>
> **DECLARATION:** Place your hand on your heart and say . . .

"I release my nonsupportive money experiences from the past and create a new and rich future."

Touch your head and say . . .

"I have a millionaire mind!"

So What Is Your Money Blueprint Set For?

Now, it's time to answer the "million dollar" question. What is your current money and success blueprint, and what results is it subconsciously moving you toward? Are you set for success, mediocrity, or financial failure? Are you programmed for struggle or for ease around money? Are you set for working hard for your money or working in balance?

Are you conditioned for having a consistent income or an inconsistent income? You know the scoop: "First you have it, then you don't, then you have it, then you don't." It always appears as though the reasons for these drastic fluctuations come from the outside world. For instance: "I got a great-paying job but then the company folded. Then I started my own business and things were booming, but the market dried up. My next business was doing super, but then my partner left, et cetera." Don't be fooled, this is your blueprint at work.

Are you set for having a high income, a moderate income, or a low income? Did you know there are actual dollar amounts for which many of us are programmed? Are you set for earning $20,000 to $30,000 a year? $40,000 to $60,000? $75,000 to $100,000? $150,000 to $200,000? $250,000 a year or more?

A few years ago, I had an unusually well-dressed gentleman in the audience during one of my two-hour evening seminars. When the seminar was complete, he came over and asked if I thought the three-day Millionaire Mind course could do anything for him, considering he was already earning $500,000 a year. I asked him how long he'd earned that kind of money. He responded, "Consistently, for about seven years now."

That was all I needed to hear. I asked him why he wasn't earning $2 million a year. I told him that the program was for people who want to reach their *full financial potential* and asked him to consider why he was "stuck" at half a million. He decided to come to the program.

I got an e-mail from him a year later that said, "The program was incredible but I made a mistake. I only reset my money blueprint to earn the $2 million a year as we discussed. I'm already there, so I'm attending the course again to reset it for earning $10 million a year."

The point I want to make is that the actual amounts don't matter. What matters is whether you are reaching your full financial potential. I know many of you might be asking, why on earth would anyone need that kind of money? First, that very question is not overly supportive to your wealth and is a sure sign you'll want to revise your money blueprint. Second, the main reason this gentleman wanted to earn massive amounts of money was to support his work as a huge donor to a charity that assists AIDS victims in Africa. So much for the belief that rich people are "greedy"!

Let's go on. Are you programmed for saving money or for spending money? Are you programmed for managing your money well or mismanaging it?

Are you set for picking winning investments or picking losers? You might wonder, "How could whether or not I make money in the stock market or in real estate be part of my blueprint?" Simple. Who picks the stock or the property? You do. Who picks when you buy it? You do. Who picks when you sell it? You do. I guess you've got something to do with the equation.

I have an acquaintance in San Diego named Larry. Larry is a magnet when it comes to making money: he definitely has a *high income* blueprint. But he has the kiss of death when it comes to investing his money. Whatever he buys drops like a rock. (Would you believe his dad had the exact same problem? Duh!) I keep in close touch with Larry so I can ask him for investment advice. It is always perfect . . . perfectly wrong! Whatever Larry suggests, I go the other way. I love Larry!

On the other hand, notice how other people seem to have what we termed earlier the Midas touch. Everything they get involved with turns to gold. Both the Midas-touch and the kiss-of-death syndromes are nothing more than the manifestations of money blueprints.

Once again, your money blueprint will determine your financial life—and even your personal life. If you are a woman whose money blueprint is set for low, chances are you will attract a man who is also set for low so you can stay in your financial "comfort zone" and validate your blueprint. If you are a man who is set for low, chances are you will attract a woman who is a spender and gets rid of all your money, so you can stay in your financial "comfort zone" and validate your blueprint.

Most people believe the success of their business is primarily dependent on their business skills and knowledge or at least their timing of the marketplace. I hate to be the one to break it to you, but that's la-la land, which is another way of saying, not a chance!

How well your business does is a result of your money blueprint. You will always validate your blueprint. If you have a blueprint that is set for earning $100,000 a year, that's exactly how well the business will do, enough to earn you about $100,000 a year.

If you are a salesperson and your blueprint is set for earning $50,000 a year and somehow you make a huge sale that makes you $90,000 that year, either the sale will cancel or if you do end up with $90,000, get ready for a crummy year to follow to make up for it and bring you back to the level of your financial blueprint.

On the other hand, if you're set for earning $50,000 and you've been in a slump for a couple of years, don't worry, you'll get it all back. You have to, it's the subconscious law of the mind and money. Someone in this position would probably walk across the street, get hit by a bus, and end up with exactly $50,000 a year in insurance! It's simple: one way or another, if you're set for $50,000 a year, eventually that's what you'll get.

So again, how can you tell what your money blueprint is set for? One of the most obvious ways is to look at your results. Look at your bank account. Look at your income. Look at your net worth. Look at your success with investments. Look at your business success. Look at whether you're a spender or a saver. Look at whether you manage money well. Look at how consistent or inconsistent you are. Look at how hard you work for your money. Look at your relationships that involve money.

Is money a struggle or does it come to you easily? Do you own a business or do you have a job? Do you stick with one business or job for a long time or do you jump around a lot?

Your blueprint is like a thermostat. If the temperature in

the room is seventy-two degrees, chances are good that the thermostat is set for seventy-two degrees. Now here's where it gets interesting. Is it possible that because the window is open and it is cold outside, the temperature in the room can drop to sixty-five degrees? Of course, but what will eventually happen? The thermostat will kick in and bring the temperature back to seventy-two.

Also, is it possible that because the window is open and it's hot outside, the temperature in the room can go up to seventy-seven degrees? Sure it could, but what will eventually happen? The thermostat will kick in and bring the temperature back to seventy-two.

The only way to permanently change the temperature in the room is to reset the thermostat. In the same way, the only way to change your level of financial success "permanently" is to reset your financial thermostat, otherwise known as your money blueprint.

WEALTH PRINCIPLE:
The only way to permanently change the temperature in the room is to reset the thermostat. In the same way, the only way to change your level of financial success "permanently" is to reset your financial thermostat.

You can try anything and everything else you want. You can develop your knowledge in business, in marketing, in sales, in negotiations, and in management. You can become an expert in real estate or the stock market. All of these are tremendous "tools." But in the end, without an inner "toolbox" that is big enough and strong enough for you to create and hold on to large amounts of money, all the tools in the world will be useless to you.

Once again, it's simple arithmetic: "Your income can grow only to the extent that you do."

Fortunately or unfortunately, your personal money and success blueprint will tend to stay with you for the rest of your life—unless you identify and change it. And that is exactly what we will continue to do in Part II of this book and do even further with you at the Millionaire Mind Intensive Seminar.

Remember that the first element of all change is awareness. Watch yourself, become conscious, observe your thoughts, your fears, your beliefs, your habits, your actions, and even your inactions. Put yourself under a microscope. Study yourself.

Most of us believe that we live our lives based on choice. Not usually! Even if we're really enlightened, we might make just a few choices during the average day that reflect our awareness of ourselves in the present moment. But for the most part, we're like robots, running on automatic, ruled by our past conditioning and old habits. That's where consciousness comes in. Consciousness is observing your thoughts and actions so that you can live from true choice in the present moment rather than being run by programming from the past.

WEALTH PRINCIPLE:
Consciousness is observing your thoughts
and actions so that you can live from true choice
in the present moment rather than being
run by programming from the past.

By achieving consciousness, we can live from who we are today rather than who we were yesterday. In this way, we can respond appropriately to situations, tapping the full range and potential of our skills and talents, rather than inappropriately reacting to events, driven by the fears and insecurities of the past.

Once you are conscious, you can see your programming for what it is: simply a recording of information you received and believed in the past, when you were too young to know any better. You can see that this conditioning is not who you are but who you learned to be. You can see that you are not the "recording" but the "recorder." You are not the "content" in the glass but the "glass" itself. You are not the software but the hardware.

Yes, genetics may play a role, and, yes, spiritual aspects may come into play, but much of what shapes who you are comes from other people's beliefs and information. As I suggested earlier, beliefs are not necessarily true or false or right or wrong, but regardless of their validity, beliefs are opinions that are passed around and around and then down from generation to generation to you. Knowing this, you can consciously choose to release any belief or way of being that is not supportive to your wealth, and you can replace it with one that is.

In our courses we teach that "no thought lives in your head rent-free." Each thought you have will either be an investment or a cost. It will either move you toward happiness and success or away from it. It will either empower you or disempower you. That's why it is imperative you choose your thoughts and beliefs wisely.

Realize that your thoughts and beliefs aren't who you are, and they are not necessarily attached to you. As precious as you believe them to be, they have no more importance and meaning than you give them. *Nothing has meaning except for the meaning you give it.*

Recall how at the beginning of this book I suggested you don't believe a word I say? Well, if you really want to take off in your life, don't believe a word *you* say. And if you want instant enlightenment, *don't believe a thought you think.*

Meanwhile, if you're like most people, you're going to believe something, so you might as well adopt beliefs that support you, rich beliefs. Remember, thoughts lead to feelings, which lead to actions, which lead to results. You can choose to think and act like rich people do and therefore create the results that rich people create.

The question is, "How do rich people think and act?" That's exactly what you'll discover in Part II of this book.

If you want to change your financial life forever, read on!

DECLARATION: Place your hand on your heart and say . . .

"I observe my thoughts and entertain only those that empower me."

Touch your head and say . . .

"I have a millionaire mind!"

Success Story from Rhonda & Bob Baines

From: Rhonda & Bob Baines
To: T. Harv Eker
Subject: We feel free!

We went to the Millionaire Mind Intensive not really knowing what to expect. We were very impressed with the results. Before attending the seminar, we were having a lot of money problems. We never seemed to get ahead. We would continually be in debt and not know why. We would pay off our credit cards (usually from a large bonus at work), only to get back into debt within six months. It did not matter how much money we made. We were very frustrated and argued a lot.

Then we attended Millionaire Mind. While listening to Harv, my husband and I kept squeezing each other's leg and smiling and looking at each other. We heard so much information that had us saying, "No wonder," "Oh, so that's why," "Everything makes sense now." We were very excited.

We learned how he and I think so differently when it comes to money. How he is a "spender" and how I am an "avoider." What a horrible combination! After hearing the information, we stopped blaming each other and started understanding each other and ultimately started to appreciate and love each other more.

It is almost a year later and we still do not argue about money—we just talk about what we learned. We are no longer in debt; in fact we have money in savings, the first time in our 16-year relationship—yeah! We now not only have money for our future, but we also have enough money for our normal everyday expenses, playing, education, long-term savings for a home, and we even have money to share and give away. It feels wonderful knowing that we can use money in those areas and not feel guilty because we allocated and dedicated it for that purpose.

We feel free.

Thank you very much, Harv.

PART TWO

The Wealth Files

Seventeen Ways Rich People Think
and Act Differently from Poor
and Middle-Class People

I N PART I OF THIS BOOK WE DISCUSSED THE PROCESS of Manifestation. Recall that thoughts lead to feelings, feelings lead to actions, and actions lead to results. Everything begins with your thoughts—which are produced by your mind. Isn't it amazing that our mind is pretty much the basis for our life and yet most of us have no clue as to how this powerful apparatus functions? So let's start by taking a simple look at how your mind works. Metaphorically, your mind is nothing more than a big file cabinet, similar to what you'd find in your office or home. All information that comes in is labeled and filed in folders so that it's easy to retrieve to help you survive. Did you hear that? I didn't say *thrive,* I said *survive.*

In every situation, you go to the files of your mind to determine how to respond. Say, for example, you're considering a financial opportunity. You automatically go to your file labeled *money* and from there decide what to do. The only thoughts you can have about money will be what are stored in your money file. That's all you can think about, because that's all that is in your mind under that category.

You decide based on what you believe is logical, sensible, and appropriate for you at the time. You make what you think is the *right* choice. The problem, however, is that your right choice may not be a successful choice. In fact, what makes perfect sense to you may consistently produce perfectly poor results.

For instance, let's say my wife is in the mall. That shouldn't be too hard for me to imagine. She sees this green purse. It's on sale for 25 percent off. She immediately goes to her mind files with the question "Should I get this purse?" In a nanosecond, her mind files come back with the answer: "You've been looking for a green purse to go with those green shoes you bought last week. Plus it's just the right size. Buy it!" As she rushes to the checkout counter, her mind is not only thrilled that she's going to have this beautiful purse, but glowing with pride that she got it for 25 percent off.

To her mind, this purchase makes perfect sense. She wants it, she believes she needs it, and it is "such a deal." However, at no point did her mind come up with the thought "True, this is a really nice purse, and true, this is a great deal, but right now I'm three thousand dollars in debt, so I'd better hold off."

She didn't come up with that information because no file in her head contains that. The file of "When you're in debt, don't buy any more" was never installed in her and doesn't exist, which means that particular choice is not an option.

Do you catch my drift? If you've got files in your cabinet that are nonsupportive to financial success, those will be the only choices you can make. They'll be natural, automatic, and make perfect sense to you. But in the end, they will still produce financial failure or mediocrity at best. Conversely, if you've got mind files that support financial success, you will naturally and automatically make decisions that produce success. You won't have to think about it. Your normal way of thinking will result in success, kind of like Donald Trump. His normal way of thinking produces wealth.

When it comes to money, wouldn't it be incredible if you could inherently think how rich people think? I sure hope you said "absolutely" or something to that effect.

Well, you can!

As we stated previously, the first step to any change is awareness, meaning the first step to thinking the way rich people think is to know how rich people think.

Rich people think very differently from poor and middle-class people. They think differently about money, wealth, themselves, other people, and pretty well every other facet of life. In Part II of this book, we're going to examine some of these differences and, as part of your reconditioning, install seventeen alternative "wealth files" into your mind. With new files come new choices. You can then catch yourself when you are thinking like poor and middle-class people and consciously shift your focus to how rich people think. Remember, you can *choose* to think in ways that will support you in your happiness and success instead of ways that don't.

WEALTH PRINCIPLE:
You can choose to think in ways that will
support you in your happiness and success
instead of ways that don't.

A few caveats to begin. First, in no way, shape, or form do I mean to degrade poor people or want to appear to be without compassion for their situation. I do not believe that rich people are *better* than poor people. They're just richer. At the same time, I want to make sure you get the message, so I'm going to make the distinctions between the rich and poor as extreme as possible.

Second, when I discuss rich, poor, and middle-class people, what I am referring to is their *mentality*—how different folks think and act rather than the actual amount of money they've got or their value to society.

Third, I will be generalizing "big time." I understand that not all rich and not all poor people are the way I'm describing them to be. Again, my objective is to make sure you get the point of each principle and use it.

Fourth, for the most part, I will not always be referring to the middle class specifically, because middle-class people usually have a mix of rich and poor mentalities. Again, my goal is for you to become aware of where you fit on the scale and to think more like the rich if you want to create more wealth.

Fifth, several of the principles in this section may appear to deal more with habits and actions than with ways of thinking. Remember, our actions come from our feelings, which come from our thoughts. Consequently, every rich action is preceded by a rich way of thinking.

Finally, I'm going to ask you to be willing to let go of being *right*! What I mean by that is, be willing to let go of having to do it *your* way. Why? Because your way has gotten you exactly what you've got right now. If you want more of the same, keep doing it your way. If you're not yet rich, however, maybe it's time you consider a different way, especially one that comes from someone who is really, really rich and has put thousands of others on the road to wealth too. It's up to you.

The concepts you are about to learn are simple but profound. They make real changes for real people in the real world. How do I know? At my company, Peak Potentials Training, we get thousands of letters and e-mails each year telling us how each individual wealth file has transformed people's lives. If you learn them and use them, I am confident they will transform your life too.

At the end of each section you will find a declaration and a physical movement with which to "anchor" it into your body.

You will also find actions to take to support you in adopting this wealth file. It is imperative you put each file into action in your life as quickly as possible so that the knowledge can move to a physical, cellular level and create lasting and permanent change.

Most people understand we are creatures of habit, but what they don't realize is that there are actually two kinds of habits: *doing* habits and *not-doing* habits. Everything you are *not doing* right now, you are in the *habit* of not doing. The only way to change these not-doing habits into doing habits is to *do* them. Reading will assist you, but it's a whole different world when you go from reading to doing. If you are truly serious about success, prove it, and do the actions suggested.

Wealth File #1

**Rich people believe "I create my life."
Poor people believe "Life happens to me."**

If you want to create wealth, it is imperative that you believe that you are at the steering wheel of your life, especially your financial life. If you don't believe this, then you must inherently believe that you have little or no control over your life, and therefore you have little or no control over your financial success. That is not a rich attitude.

Did you ever notice that it's usually poor people who spend a fortune playing the lottery? They actually believe their wealth is going to come from someone picking their name out of a hat. They spend Saturday night glued to the TV, excitedly watching the draw, to see if wealth is going to "land" on them this week.

Sure, everyone wants to win the lottery, and even rich people play for fun once in a while. But first, they don't spend half their paycheck on tickets, and second, winning the lotto is not their primary "strategy" for creating wealth.

You have to believe that you are the one who creates your success, that you are the one who creates your mediocrity, and that you are the one creating your struggle around money and success. Consciously or unconsciously, it's still you.

Instead of taking responsibility for what's going on in their lives, poor people choose to play the role of the victim. A victim's predominant thought is often "poor me." So presto, by virtue of the law of intention, that's literally what victims get: they get to be "poor."

Notice that I said they play the *role* of victim. I didn't say they are victims. I don't believe anyone is a victim. I believe people play the victim because they think it gets them something. We'll discuss this in more detail shortly.

That said, how can you tell when people are playing the victim? They leave three obvious clues.

Now, before we talk about these clues, I want you to realize that I fully understand that none of these ways of being has anything to do with anyone reading this book. But maybe, just maybe, you might know someone who can relate. And maybe, just maybe, you might know that person intimately! Either way, I suggest you pay close attention to this section.

Victim Clue #1: Blame

When it comes to why they're not rich, most victims are professionals at the "blame game." The object of this game is to see how many people and circumstances you can point the finger at without ever looking at yourself. It's fun for victims at least. Unfortunately it's not such a blast for anyone else who is unlucky enough to be around them. That's because those in close proximity to victims become easy targets.

Victims blame the economy, they blame the government, they blame the stock market, they blame their broker, they blame their type of business, they blame their employer, they blame their employees, they blame their manager, they blame the head office, they blame their up-line or their down-line, they blame customer service, they blame the shipping department, they blame their partner, they blame their spouse, they blame God, and of course they always blame their parents. It's always someone else or something else that is to blame. The problem is anything or anyone but them.

Victim Clue #2: Justifying

If victims aren't blaming, you'll often find them justifying or rationalizing their situation by saying something like "Money's not really important." Let me ask you this question: If you said that your husband or your wife, or your boyfriend or your girlfriend, or your partner or your friend, weren't all that important, would any of them be around for long? I don't think so, and neither would money!

At my live seminars, some participants always come up to me and say, "You know, Harv, money's not really that important." I look them directly in the eyes and say, "You're broke! Right?" They usually look down at their feet and meekly reply with something like "Well, right now I'm having a few financial challenges, but . . ." I interrupt, "No, it's not just right now, it's always; you've always been broke or close to it, yes or yes?" At this point they usually nod their head in agreement and woefully return to their seats, ready to listen and learn, as they finally realize what a disastrous effect this one belief has had on their lives.

Of course they're broke. Would you have a motorcycle if it wasn't important to you? Of course not. Would you have a pet parrot if it wasn't important to you? Of course not. In the same way, if you don't think money is important, you simply won't have any.

You can actually dazzle your friends with this insight. Imagine you're in a conversation with a friend who tells you, "Money's not important." Put your hand on your forehead and look up as though you are getting a message from the heavens, then exclaim, "You're broke!" To which your shocked friend will undoubtedly respond, "How did you know?" Then you stretch out your palm and you reply,

"What else do you want to know? That'll be fifty bucks, please!"

Let me put it bluntly: anyone who says money isn't important doesn't have any! Rich people understand the importance of money and the place it has in our society. On the other hand, poor people validate their financial ineptitude by using irrelevant comparisons. They'll argue, "Well, money isn't as important as love." Now, is that comparison dumb or what? What's more important, your arm or your leg? Maybe they're *both* important.

Listen up, my friends: Money is extremely important in the areas in which it works, and extremely unimportant in the areas in which it doesn't. And although love may make the world go round, it sure doesn't pay for the building of any hospitals, churches, or homes. It also doesn't feed anybody.

WEALTH PRINCIPLE:
Money is extremely important in the areas
in which it works, and extremely unimportant
in the areas in which it doesn't.

Not convinced? Try paying your bills with love. Still not sure? Then pop on over to the bank and try depositing some love and see what happens. I'll save you the trouble. The teller will look at you as if you've just gone AWOL from the loony bin and scream only one word: *"Security!"*

No rich people believe money is not important. And if I've failed to persuade you and you still somehow believe that money's not important, then I have only two words for you, *you're broke,* and you always will be until you eradicate that nonsupportive file from your financial blueprint.

Victim Clue #3: Complaining

Complaining is the absolute worst possible thing you could do for your health or your wealth. The worst! Why?

I'm a big believer in the universal law that states, "What you focus on expands." When you are complaining, what are you focusing on, what's right with your life or what's wrong with it? You are obviously focusing on what's wrong with it, and since what you focus on expands, you'll keep getting more of what's wrong.

Many teachers in the personal development field talk about the Law of Attraction. It states that "like attracts like," meaning that when you are complaining, you are actually attracting "crap" into your life.

WEALTH PRINCIPLE:
When you are complaining, you become
a living, breathing "crap magnet."

Have you ever noticed that complainers usually have a tough life? It seems that everything that could go wrong does go wrong for them. They say, "Of course I complain— look how crappy my life is." And now that you know better, you can explain to them, "No, it's *because* you complain that your life is so crappy. Shut up . . . and don't stand near me!"

Which brings us to another point. You have to make darn sure not to put yourself in the proximity of complainers. If you absolutely have to be nearby, make sure you bring a steel umbrella or the crap meant for them will get you too!

I stay as far away from complainers as possible because negative energy is infectious. Plenty of people, however, love to hang out and listen to complainers. Why? It's simple: they're waiting for their turn! "You think that's bad? Wait till you hear what happened to me!"

Here's some homework that I promise will change your life. For the next seven days, I challenge you to not complain at all. Not just out loud, but in your head as well. But you have to do it for the full seven days. Why? Because for the first few days, you may still have some "residual crap" coming to you from before. Unfortunately, crap doesn't travel at the speed of light, you know, it travels at the speed of crap, so it might take a while to clear out.

I've given this challenge to thousands of people, and I'm blown away at how many of them have told me that this one, teensy-weensy exercise has transformed their lives. I guarantee you'll be astonished at how amazing your life will be when you stop focusing on—and thereby stop attracting—crap into your life. If you've been a complainer, forget about attracting success for now; for most people, just getting to "neutral" would be a great start!

Blame, justification, and complaining are like pills. They are nothing more than stress reducers. They alleviate the stress of failure. Think about it. If a person weren't failing in some way, shape, or form, would he or she need to blame, justify, or complain? The obvious answer is no.

From now on, as you hear yourself disastrously blaming, justifying, or complaining, cease and desist immediately. Remind yourself that you are creating your life and that at every moment you will be attracting either success or crap into your life. It is imperative you choose your thoughts and words wisely!

Now you're ready to hear one of the greatest secrets in the world. Are you ready? Read this carefully: *There is no such thing as a really rich victim!* Did you get that? I'll say it again: There is no such thing as a really rich victim. Besides, who would listen? "Tsk, tsk, I got a scratch in my yacht." To which almost anyone would respond, "Who gives a hoot?"

WEALTH PRINCIPLE:
There is no such thing as a really rich victim!

Meanwhile, being a victim definitely has its rewards. What do people get out of being a victim? The answer is *attention.* Is attention important? You bet it is. In some form or another it's what almost everyone lives for. And the reason people live for attention is that they've made a critical mistake. It is the same error that virtually all of us have made. We've confused attention with love.

Believe me, it is virtually impossible to be truly happy and successful when you're constantly yearning for attention. Because if it's attention you want, you're at the mercy of others. You usually end up as a "people pleaser" begging for approval. Attention-seeking is also a problem because people tend to do stupid things to get it. It is imperative to "unhook" attention and love, for a number of reasons.

First, you will be more successful; second, you will be happier; and third, you can find "true" love in your life. For the most part, when people confuse love and attention, they don't love each other in the true spiritual sense of the word. They love each other largely from the place of their own ego, as in "I love what you do for me." Therefore, the relationship is really about the individual, and not about the other person or at least the both of you.

By disconnecting attention from love, you will be freed

up to love another for who they *are,* rather than what they do for you.

Now, as I said, there is no such thing as a rich victim. So to stay a victim, attention seekers make darn sure they never get rich.

It's time to decide. You can be a victim *or* you can be rich, but you can't be both. Listen up! Every time, and I mean *every* time, you blame, justify, or complain, you are *slitting your financial throat.* Sure, it would be nice to use a kinder and gentler metaphor, but forget it. I'm not interested in kind or gentle right now. I'm interested in helping you see exactly what the heck you're doing to yourself! Later, once you get rich, we can be kinder and gentler, how's that?

It's time to take back your power and acknowledge that you create everything that is in your life and everything that is not in it. Realize that you create your wealth, your non-wealth, and every level in between.

DECLARATION: Place your hand on your heart and say . . .

"I create the exact level of my financial success!"

Touch your head and say . . .

"I have a millionaire mind!"

MILLIONAIRE MIND ACTIONS

1. Every time you catch yourself blaming, justifying, or complaining, slide your index finger across your neck, as a *trigger* to remind yourself that you are slitting your financial throat. Once again, even though this gesture may seem a little crude to do to yourself, it's no more crude than what you're doing to yourself by blaming,

justifying, or complaining, and it will eventually work to alleviate these destructive habits.

2. Do a "debrief." At the end of each day, write down one thing that went well and one thing that didn't. Then write the answer to the following question: "How did I create each of these situations?" If others were involved, ask yourself, "What was my part in creating each of these situations?" This exercise will keep you accountable for your life and make you aware of the strategies that are working for you and the strategies that are not.

Special Bonus: Go to **www.millionairemindbook.com** and click on "FREE BOOK BONUSES" to receive your free Millionaire Mind "action reminders."

Wealth File #2

Rich people play the money game to win. Poor people play the money game to *not* lose.

Poor people play the money game on defense rather than offense. Let me ask you: If you were to play any sport or any game strictly on defense, what are the chances of your winning that game? Most people would agree, slim and none.

Yet that's exactly how most people play the money game. Their primary concern is survival and security instead of creating wealth and abundance. So, what is your goal? What is your objective? What is your true intention?

The goal of truly rich people is to have massive wealth and abundance. Not just some money, but lots of money. So what is the big goal of poor people? To "have enough to pay the bills . . . and on time would be a miracle!" Again, let me remind you of the power of intention. When your intention is to have enough to pay the bills, that's exactly how much you'll get—just enough to pay the bills and not a dime more.

Middle-class people at least go a step further . . . too bad it's a tiny step. Their big goal in life also happens to be their favorite word in the whole wide world. They just want to be "comfortable." I hate to break the news to you, but there's a huge difference between being comfortable and being rich.

I have to admit, I didn't always know that. But one of the reasons I believe I have the right to even write this book is that I've had the experience of being on all three sides of the proverbial fence. I've been extremely broke, as in having to borrow a dollar for gas for my car. But let me qualify that. First, it wasn't my car. Second, that dollar came in the form of four quarters. Do you know how embarrassing it is for an adult to pay for gas with four quarters? The kid at the pump looked at me as if I were some kind of vending-machine robber and then just shook his head and laughed. I don't know if you can relate, but it was definitely one of my financial low points and unfortunately just one of them.

Once I got my act together, I graduated to the level of being *comfortable.* Comfortable is nice. At least you go out to decent restaurants for a change. But pretty much all I could order was chicken. Now, there's nothing wrong with chicken, if that's what you really want. But often it's not.

In fact, people who are only financially comfortable usually decide on what to eat by looking at the right-hand side of the menu—the price side. "What would you like for dinner tonight, dear?" "I'll have this $7.95 dish. Let's see what it is. Surprise, surprise, it's the chicken," for the nineteenth time this week!

When you're comfortable, you don't dare allow your eyes to look at the bottom of the menu, for if you did, you might come across the most forbidden words in the middle-class dictionary: *market price*! And even if you were curious, you'd never ask what the price actually is. First, because you know you can't afford it. Second, it's downright embarrassing when you know the waiter doesn't believe you when he tells you the dish is $49 with side dishes extra and you say, "You know what, for some reason, I have a real craving for chicken tonight!"

I have to say that for me personally, one of the best things about being rich is not having to look at the prices on the menu anymore. I eat exactly what I want to eat regardless of the price. I can assure you, I didn't do that when I was *broke* or *comfortable.*

It boils down to this: If your goal is to be comfortable, chances are you'll never get rich. But if your goal is to be rich, chances are you'll end up mighty comfortable.

WEALTH PRINCIPLE:
If your goal is to be comfortable, chances are you'll never get rich. But if your goal is to be rich, chances are you'll end up mighty comfortable.

One of the principles we teach in our programs is "If you shoot for the stars, you'll at least hit the moon." Poor people don't even shoot for the ceiling in their house, and then they wonder why they're not successful. Well, they just found out. You get what you truly intend to get. If you want to get rich, your goal has to be rich. Not to have enough to pay the bills, and not just to have enough to be comfortable. Rich means rich!

DECLARATION: Place your hand on your heart and say . . .

"My goal is to become a millionaire and more!"

Touch your head and say . . .

"I have a millionaire mind!"

MILLIONAIRE MIND ACTIONS

1. Write down two financial objectives that demonstrate your intention to create abundance, not mediocrity or poverty. Write "play to win" goals for your:

   a. Annual income

   b. Net worth

   Make these goals achievable with a realistic time frame, yet at the same time remember to "shoot for the stars."

2. Go to an upscale restaurant and order a meal at "market price" without asking how much it costs. (If funds are tight, sharing is acceptable.)

   P.S. No chicken!

Wealth File #3

Rich people are committed to being rich. Poor people want to be rich.

Ask most people if they want to be rich and they'd look at you as if you were crazy. "Of course I want to be rich," they'd say. The truth, however, is that most people don't really want to be rich. Why? Because they have a lot of negative wealth files in their subconscious mind that tell them there is something wrong with being rich.

At our Millionaire Mind Intensive Seminar, one of the questions we ask people is "What are some of the possible negatives about being rich or trying to get rich?"

Here's what some people have to say. See if you can relate to any of these.

"What if I make it and lose it? Then I'll really be a failure."

"I'll never know if people like me for myself or for my money."

"I'll be at the highest tax bracket and have to give half my money to the government."

"It's too much work."

"I could lose my health trying."

"My friends and family will say, 'Who do you think you are?' and criticize me."

"Everyone's going to want a handout."

"I could be robbed."

"My kids could be kidnapped."

"It's too much responsibility. I'll have to manage all that money. I'll have to really understand investments. I'll have to worry about tax strategies and asset protection and have to hire expensive accountants and lawyers. Yuck, what a hassle."

And on and on it goes. . . .

As I mentioned earlier, each of us has a wealth file inside the cabinet called our mind. This file contains our personal beliefs that include why being rich would be wonderful. However, for many people, this file also includes information as to why being rich might not be so wonderful. This means they have mixed internal messages about wealth. One part of them gleefully says, "Having more money will make life a lot more fun." But then another part screams, "Yeah, but I'm going to have to work like a dog! What fun is that?" One part says, "I'll be able to travel the world." Then the other part chirps in, "Yeah, and everyone in the world will want a handout." These mixed messages may seem innocent enough, but in reality, they are one of the major reasons most people never become rich.

You can look at it like this. The universe, which is another way of saying "higher power," is akin to a big mail-order department. It is constantly delivering people, events, and things to you. You "order" what you get by sending energetic messages out to the universe based on your predominant beliefs. Again, based on the Law of Attraction, the universe will do its best to say yes and support you. But if you have mixed messages in your file, the universe can't understand what you want.

One minute the universe hears that you want to be rich, so it begins sending you opportunities for wealth. But then it hears you say, "Rich people are greedy," so the universe begins to support you in not having much money. But then you think, "Having a lot of money makes life so much more enjoyable," so the poor universe, dazed and confused, restarts sending you opportunities for more money. The next day you're in an uninspired mood so you think, "Money's not that important." The frustrated universe finally screams, "Make up your frickin' mind! I'll get you what you want, just tell me what it is!"

The number one reason most people don't get what they want is that they don't know what they want. Rich people are totally clear that they want wealth. They are unwavering in their desire. They are fully committed to creating wealth. As long as it's legal, moral, and ethical, they will do *whatever it takes* to have wealth. Rich people do not send mixed messages to the universe. Poor people do.

(By the way, when you read that last paragraph, if a little voice inside your head said something to the effect of "Rich people don't care if it's legal, moral, or ethical," you are definitely doing the right thing in reading this book. You'll soon find out what a detrimental way of thinking that is.)

WEALTH PRINCIPLE:
The number one reason most people
don't get what they want is that they
don't know what they want.

Poor people have plenty of good reasons as to why getting and actually being rich might be a problem. Consequently, they are not 100 percent certain they really want to be rich. Their message to the universe is confusing. Their message to others is confusing. And why does all of this confusion happen? Because their message to themselves is confusing.

Earlier we talked about the power of intention. I know it might be hard to believe, but you always get what you want—what you *subconsciously* want, not what you *say* you want. You might emphatically deny this and respond, "That's crazy! Why would I want to struggle?" And my question for you is exactly the same: "I don't know. Why would you want to struggle?"

If you want to discover the reason, I invite you to attend the Millionaire Mind Intensive Seminar, where you will identify your money blueprint. The answer will be staring you in the face. Put bluntly, if you are not achieving the wealth you say you desire, there's a good chance it's because, first, you subconsciously don't really want wealth, or second, you're not willing to do what it takes to create it.

Let's explore this further. There are actually three levels of so-called wanting. The first level is "I *want* to be rich." That's another way of saying, "I'll take it if it falls in my lap." Wanting alone is useless. Have you noticed that wanting doesn't necessarily lead to "having"? Notice also that wanting without having leads to more wanting. Wanting becomes habitual and leads only to itself, creating a perfect circle that goes exactly nowhere. Wealth does not come from merely wanting it. How do you know this is true? With a simple reality check: billions of people *want* to be rich, relatively few are.

The second level of wanting is "I *choose* to be rich." This entails deciding to become rich. Choosing is a much stronger energy and goes hand in hand with being responsible for creating your reality. The word *decision* comes from the Latin word *decidere,* which means "to kill off any other alternatives." Choosing is better but not best.

The third level of wanting is "I *commit* to being rich." The definition of the word *commit* is "to devote oneself unreservedly." This means holding absolutely nothing back; giving 100 percent of everything you've got to achieving wealth. It means being willing to do whatever it takes for as long as it takes. This is the warrior's way. No excuses, no ifs, no buts, no maybes—and failure is not an option. The warrior's way is simple: "I will be rich or I will die trying."

"I commit to being rich." Try saying that to yourself. . . . What comes up for you? For some, it feels empowering. For others, it feels daunting.

Most people would never truly commit to being rich. If you asked them, "Would you bet your life that in the next ten years you will be wealthy?" most would say, "No way!" That's the difference between rich people and poor people. It's precisely because people won't truly commit to being rich that they are not rich and most likely never will be.

Some might say, "Harv, what are you talking about? I work my butt off, I'm trying real hard. Of course I'm committed to being rich." And I would reply, "That you're trying means little. The definition of *commitment* is to devote oneself unreservedly." The key word is *unreservedly*. Which means you're putting everything, and I mean everything, you've got into it. Most people I know who are not financially successful have limits on how much they are willing to do, how much they are willing to risk, and how much they are willing to sacrifice. Although they think they're willing to do whatever it takes, upon deeper questioning I always find they have plenty of conditions around what they are willing to do and not do to succeed!

I hate to have to be the one to tell you this, but getting rich is not a stroll in the park, and anyone who tells you it is either knows a heck of a lot more than me or is a little out of integrity. In my experience, getting rich takes focus, courage, knowledge, expertise, 100 percent of your effort, a never-give-up attitude, and of course a rich mind-set. You also have to believe in your heart of hearts that you can create wealth and that you absolutely deserve it. Again, what this means is that, if you are not fully, totally, and truly committed to creating wealth, chances are you won't.

WEALTH PRINCIPLE:
If you are not fully, totally, and truly committed
to creating wealth, chances are you won't.

Are you willing to work sixteen hours a day? Rich people are. Are you willing to work seven days a week and give up most of your weekends? Rich people are. Are you willing to sacrifice seeing your family, your friends, and give up your recreations and hobbies? Rich people are. Are you willing to risk all your time, energy, and start-up capital with no guarantee of returns? Rich people are.

For a time, hopefully a short time but often a long time, rich people are ready and willing to do all of the above. Are you?

Maybe you'll be lucky and you won't have to work long or hard or sacrifice anything. You can wish for that, but I sure wouldn't count on it. Again, rich people are committed enough to do whatever it takes. Period.

It's interesting to note, however, that once you do commit, the universe will bend over backward to support you. One of my favorite passages is by explorer W. H. Murray, who wrote the following during one of the first Himalayan expeditions:

> *Until one is committed, there is hesitancy, the chance to draw back, always ineffectiveness. Concerning all acts of initiative (and creation), there is one elementary truth, the ignorance of which kills countless ideas and splendid plans: that the moment one definitely commits oneself, then providence moves too. A whole stream of events issues from the decision, raising in one's favor all manner of unforeseen incidents, meetings, and material assistance, which no man could have dreamt would have come his way.*

In other words, the universe will assist you, guide you, support you, and even create miracles for you. But first, you have to commit!

DECLARATION: Place your hand on your heart and say . . .

"I commit to being rich."

Touch your head and say . . .

"I have a millionaire mind!"

MILLIONAIRE MIND ACTIONS

1. Write a short paragraph on exactly why creating wealth is important to you. Be specific.

2. Meet with a friend or family member who is willing to support you. Tell that person you want to evoke the power of commitment for the purpose of creating greater success. Put your hand on your heart, look that person in the eye, and repeat the following statement:

   "I, _____ [your name], do hereby commit to becoming a millionaire or more by _____ [date]."

   Tell your partner to say, "I believe in you."

   Then you say, "Thank you."

   P.S. To strengthen your commitment, I invite you to commit directly to me at **www.millionairemindbook .com,** then print out your commitment and post it on your wall.

   P.P.S. Check in as to how you feel before your commitment and how you feel after it. If you feel a sense of freedom, you're on your way. If you feel a tinge of fear, you're on your way. If you didn't bother doing it, you're still in "not being willing to do whatever it takes" mode or "I don't need to do any of this weird stuff" mode. Either way, let me remind you, *your* way has gotten you exactly where you are right now.

Wealth File #4

Rich people think big.
Poor people think small.

We once had a trainer teaching at one of our seminars who went from a net worth of $250,000 to over $600 million in only three years. When asked his secret, he said, "Everything changed the moment I began to think big." I refer you to the Law of Income, which states, "You will be paid in direct proportion to the value you deliver according to the marketplace."

WEALTH PRINCIPLE:
The Law of Income: You will be paid in direct proportion to the value you deliver according to the marketplace.

The key word is *value*. It's important to know that four factors determine your value in the marketplace: *supply, demand, quality,* and *quantity*. In my experience, the factor that presents the biggest challenge for most people is the quantity. The quantity factor simply means, how much of your value do you actually deliver to the marketplace?

Another way of stating this is, how many people do you actually serve or affect?

In my business, for instance, some trainers prefer teaching small groups of twenty people at a time, others are comfortable with a hundred participants in the room, others like an audience of five hundred, and still others love audiences of a thousand to five thousand or more. Is there a difference in income among these trainers? You better believe there is!

Consider the network marketing business. Is there a difference in income between someone who has ten people in his or her down-line and someone who has ten thousand people? I would think so!

Near the beginning of this book, I mentioned that I owned a chain of retail fitness stores. From the moment I even considered going into this business, my intention was to have one hundred successful stores and affect tens of thousands of people. My competitor, on the other hand, who started six months after me, had the intention of owning one successful store. In the end, she earned a decent living. I got rich!

How do you want to live your life? How do you want to play the game? Do you want to play in the big leagues or in the little leagues, in the majors or the minors? Are you going to play big or play small? It's your choice.

Most people choose to play small. Why? First, because of fear. They're scared to death of failure and they're even more frightened of success. Second, people play small because they feel small. They feel unworthy. They don't feel they're good enough or important enough to make a real difference in people's lives.

But hear this: Your life is not just about you. It's also about contributing to others. It's about living true to your mission and reason for being here on this earth at this time. It's about adding your piece of the puzzle to the world. Most people are so stuck in their egos that everything revolves around me, me, and more me. But if you want to be rich in the truest sense of the word, it can't only be about you. It has to include adding value to other people's lives.

One of the greatest inventors and philosophers of our time, Buckminster Fuller, said, "The purpose of our lives is to add value to the people of this generation and those that follow."

We each came to this earth with natural talents, things we're just naturally good at. These gifts were given to you for a reason: to use and share with others. Research shows that the happiest people are those who use their natural talents to the utmost. Part of your mission in life then must be to share your gifts and value with as many people as possible. That means being willing to play big.

Do you know the definition of an entrepreneur? The definition we use in our programs is "a person who solves problems for people at a profit." That's right, an entrepreneur is nothing more than a "problem solver."

So I ask you, would you rather solve problems for more people or fewer people? If you replied more, then you need to start thinking bigger and decide to help massive numbers of people—thousands, even millions. The by-product is that the more people you help, the "richer" you become, mentally, emotionally, spiritually, and definitely financially.

Make no mistake, every person on this planet has a mission. If you are living right now, there's a reason for it. Richard Bach, in his book *Jonathan Livingston Seagull,* is asked, "How will I know when I've completed my mission?" The answer? "If you are still breathing, you are not done."

What I have witnessed is too many people not doing their *job,* not fulfilling their *duty,* or *dharma* as it's called in Sanskrit. I watch too many people playing far too small, and too many people allowing their fear-based ego selves to rule them. The result is that too many of us are not living up to our full potential, in terms of both our own lives and our contribution to others.

It comes down to this: If not you, then who?

Again, everyone has his or her unique purpose. Maybe you're a real estate investor and buy properties to rent them out and make money on cash flow and appreciation. What's your mission? How do you help? There's a good chance you add value to your community by helping families find affordable housing they may not otherwise be able to find. Now the question is how many families and people can you assist? Are you willing to help ten instead of one, twenty instead of ten, one hundred instead of twenty? This is what I mean by playing big.

In her wonderful book *A Return to Love,* author Marianne Williamson puts it this way:

> *You are a child of God. Your playing small does not serve the world. There is nothing enlightened about shrinking so that other people won't feel insecure around you. We are all meant to shine, as children do. We were born to make manifest the glory of God that is within us. It is not just in some of us; it is in everyone. And as we let our own light shine, we unconsciously give other people permission to do the same. As we are liberated from our own fear, our presence automatically liberates others.*

The world doesn't need more people playing small. It's time to stop hiding out and start stepping out. It's time to stop needing and start leading. It's time to start sharing your gifts instead of hoarding them or pretending they don't exist. It's time you started playing the game of life in a "big" way.

In the end, small thinking and small actions lead to being both broke and unfulfilled. Big thinking and big actions

---

Success Story from Jim Rosemary

From: Jim Rosemary
To: T. Harv Eker

If someone had said to me I would have doubled my income and simultaneously doubled my time off, I would have said that was not possible. But that is exactly what has happened.

In one year our business grew 175 percent, and in that same year we took a total of seven weeks of vacation time (much of that spent at additional Peak Potentials' seminars)! This is astounding considering we had experienced minimal growth over the previous five years and struggled to get even two weeks of time off a year.

As a result of knowing Harv Eker and being involved with Peak Potentials, I have a deeper understanding of myself and a greater appreciation for the abundance in my life. My relationship with my wife and children has been immeasurably enhanced. I now see more opportunities than I ever thought possible. I feel that I truly am on the right path to success in all its facets.

---

lead to having both money and meaning. The choice is yours!

DECLARATION: Place your hand on your heart and say . . .

"I think big! I choose to help thousands and thousands of people!"

Touch your head and say . . .

"I have a millionaire mind!"

MILLIONAIRE MIND ACTIONS

1. Write down what you believe to be your "natural talents." These are things you've always been naturally good at. Also write how and where you can use more of these gifts in your life and especially your work life.

2. Write down or brainstorm with a group of people how you can solve problems for ten times the number of people you affect in your job or business now. Come up with at least three different strategies. Think "leverage."

Wealth File #5

Rich people focus on opportunities. Poor people focus on obstacles.

Rich people see opportunities. Poor people see obstacles. Rich people see potential growth. Poor people see potential loss. Rich people focus on the rewards. Poor focus on the risks.

It comes down to the age-old question, "Is the glass half empty or half full?" We're not talking *positive* thinking here, we're talking about your habitual perspective on the world. Poor people make choices based upon fear. Their minds are constantly scanning for what is wrong or could go wrong in any situation. Their primary mind-set is "What if it doesn't work?" or, more often, "It won't work."

Middle-class people are slightly more optimistic. Their mind-set is "I sure hope this works."

Rich people, as we've said earlier, take responsibility for the results in their lives and act upon the mind-set "It will work because I'll make it work."

Rich people expect to succeed. They have confidence in their abilities, they have confidence in their creativity, and they believe that should the doo-doo hit the fan, they can find another way to succeed.

Generally speaking, the higher the reward, the higher the risk. Because they constantly see opportunity, rich people are willing to take a risk. Rich people believe that, if worse comes to worst, they can always make their money back.

Poor people, on the other hand, expect to fail. They lack confidence in themselves and in their abilities. Poor people believe that should things not work out, it would be catastrophic. And because they constantly see obstacles, they are usually unwilling to take a risk. No risk, no reward.

For the record, being willing to risk doesn't necessarily mean that you are willing to lose. Rich people take *educated* risks. This means that they research, do their due diligence, and make decisions based on solid information and facts. Do rich people take forever to get educated? No. They do what they can in as short a time as possible, then make an informed decision to go for it or not.

Although poor people claim to be preparing for an opportunity, what they're usually doing is *stalling*. They're scared to death, hemming and hawing for weeks, months, and even years on end, and by then the opportunity usually disappears. Then they rationalize the situation by saying, "I was getting ready." Sure enough, but while they were "getting ready," the rich guy got in, got out, and made another fortune.

I know what I'm about to say may sound a little strange considering how much I value self-responsibility. However, I do believe a certain element of what many people call luck is associated with getting rich, or, for that matter, with being successful at anything.

In football, it might be the opposing team's player fumbling on your own one-yard line with less than a minute to go, allowing your team to win the game. In golf it could be the errant shot that hits an out-of-bounds tree and bounces back onto the green, just three inches from the hole.

In business, how many times have you heard of a guy who plops some money down on a piece of land in the boonies, and ten years later, some conglomerate decides it wants to build a shopping center or office building on it? This investor gets rich. So, was it a brilliant business move on his part or sheer luck? My guess is that it's a bit of both.

The point, however, is that no luck—or anything else worthwhile—will come your way unless you take some form of *action.* To succeed financially, you have to do something, buy something, or start something. And when you do, is it luck or is it the universe or a higher power supporting you in its miraculous ways for having the courage and commitment to go for it? As far as I'm concerned, who cares what it is. It happens!

Another key principle, pertinent here, is that rich people focus on what they want, while poor people focus on what they *don't* want. Again, the universal law states, "What you focus on expands." Because rich people focus on the opportunities in everything, opportunities abound for them. Their biggest problem is handling all the incredible money-making possibilities they see. On the other hand, because poor people focus on the obstacles in everything, obstacles abound for them and their biggest problem is handling all the incredible obstacles they see.

It's simple. Your field of focus determines what you find in life. Focus on opportunities and that's what you find. Focus on obstacles and that's what you find. I'm not saying that you don't take care of problems. Of course, handle problems as they arise, in the present. But keep your eye on your goal, keep moving toward your target. Put your time and energy into creating what you want. When obstacles arise, handle them, then quickly refocus on your vision. You do not make your life about solving problems. You don't spend all your time fighting fires. Those who do, move backward! You spend your time and energy in thought and deed, moving steadily forward, toward your goal.

Do you want some simple but extremely rare advice? Here it is: If you want to get rich, focus on making, keeping, and investing your money. If you want to be poor, focus on spending your money. You can read a thousand books and take a hundred courses on success, but it all boils down to that. Remember, what you focus on expands.

Rich people also understand that you can never know all the information beforehand. In another of our programs, Enlightened Warrior Training, we train people to access their inner power and succeed in spite of anything. In this course we teach a principle known as "Ready, fire, aim!" What do we mean? Get ready the best you can in as short a time as possible; take action; then correct along the way.

It's nuts to think you can know everything that may happen in the future. It's delusional to believe you can prepare for every circumstance that might someday occur and protect yourself from it. Did you know that there are no straight lines in the universe? Life doesn't travel in perfectly straight lines. It moves more like a winding river. More often than not, you can only see to the next bend, and only when you reach that next turn can you see more.

The idea is to get in the game with whatever you've got, from wherever you are. I call this entering the *corridor.* For example, years ago I was planning on opening an all-night dessert café in Fort Lauderdale, Florida. I studied location options, the marketplace, and found out what equipment I'd need. I also researched the kinds of cakes, pies, ice creams, and coffees available. The first big problem—I got really fat! Eating my research wasn't helpful. So I asked myself, "Harv, what would be the best way to study this business?" Then I heard this guy named Harv, who was obviously a lot smarter than me, answer, "If you really want to learn a business, get into it. You don't have to own the darn thing from day one. Get in the corridor by getting a job in the arena. You'll learn more by sweeping up a restaurant and washing dishes than by ten years of research from the outside." (I told you he was a lot smarter than me.)

And that's what I did. I got a job at Mother Butler's Pie Shop. I wish I could tell you that they immediately recognized my superb talents and started me as CEO. But alas, somehow they just didn't see, nor did they care about, my executive leadership skills, and so I began as a busboy. That's right, sweeping the floor and clearing dishes. Funny how the power of intention works, isn't it?

You might think that I must really have had to swallow my pride to do this, but the truth is, I never looked at it that way. I was on a mission to learn the dessert business; I was grateful for the opportunity to learn it on someone else's "ticket" and make some pocket change to boot.

During my tenure as the pie busboy, I spent as much time as possible shootin' the doo-doo with the manager about revenues and profits, checking boxes to find out the names of the suppliers, and helping the baker at 4:00 a.m., to learn about equipment, ingredients, and problems that could occur.

A full week went by and I guess I was pretty good at my job, because the manager sat me down, fed me some pie (yuck!), and promoted me to . . . (drumroll please) *cashier*! I thought about it long and hard, for exactly a nanosecond, and replied, "Thanks but no thanks."

First, there was no way I could learn much being stuck behind a cash register. Second, I'd already learned what I came to learn. Mission accomplished!

So that's what I mean by being in the "corridor." It means entering the arena where you want to be in the future, in any capacity, to get started. This is far and away the best way to learn about a business, because you see it from the inside. Second, you can make the contacts you need, which you could never have made from the outside. Third, once you're in the corridor, many other doors of opportunity may open to you. That is, once you witness what's really going on, you may discover a niche for yourself that you hadn't recognized before. Fourth, you may find that you don't really like this field, and thank goodness you found out before you got in too deep!

So which of the above happened for me? By the time I was done with Mother Butler's, I couldn't stand the smell or sight of pie. Second, the baker quit the day after I left, phoned me, and explained that he had just found out about a hot, new piece of exercise equipment known as Gravity Guidance inversion boots (you may have seen Richard Gere hang upside down in these in the movie *American Gigolo*) and wanted to know if I was interested in looking at them. I checked things out and decided the boots were dynamite, but he wasn't, so I got involved on my own.

I began selling the boots to sporting-goods and department stores. I noticed these retail outlets all had one thing in common—crummy exercise equipment. My brain bells went berserk—"Opportunity, opportunity, opportunity." Funny how things happen. This was my first experience selling exercise equipment, which eventually led me to opening one of the first retail fitness stores in North America and making my very first million. And to think it all started with me being a busboy at Mother Butler's Pies Shop! The moral is simple: get in the corridor. You never know what doors will open unto you.

I have a motto: "Action always beats inaction." Rich people get started. They trust that once they get in the game, they can make intelligent decisions in the present moment, make corrections, and adjust their sails along the way.

Poor people don't trust in themselves or their abilities, so they believe they have to know everything in advance, which is virtually impossible. Meanwhile they don't do squat! In the end, with their positive, "ready, fire, aim," attitude, rich people take action and usually win.

In the end, by telling themselves, "I'm not doing anything until I've identified every possible problem and know exactly what to do about it," poor people never take action and therefore always lose.

Rich people see an opportunity, jump on it, and get even richer. As for poor people? They're still "preparing"!

DECLARATIONS: Place your hand on your heart and say . . .

"I focus on opportunities over obstacles."
"I get ready, I fire, I aim!"

Touch your head and say . . .

"I have a millionaire mind!"

MILLIONAIRE MIND ACTIONS

1. Get in the game. Consider a situation or project you've wanted to start. Whatever you've been waiting for, forget it. Begin now from wherever you are with whatever you've got. If possible, do it while working for or with someone else, first, to learn the ropes. If you've already learned, no more excuses. Go for it!

2. Practice optimism. Today, whatever anyone says is a problem or an obstacle, reframe it into an opportunity. You'll drive negative people nuts, but, hey, what's the difference? That's what they're constantly doing to themselves anyway!

3. Focus on what you have, not on what you don't have. Make a list of ten things you are grateful for in your life and read the list aloud. Then read it each morning for the next thirty days. If you don't appreciate what you've got, you won't get any more and you don't need any more.

Wealth File #6

Rich people admire other rich and successful people. Poor people resent rich and successful people.

Poor people often look at other people's success with resentment, jealousy, and envy. Or they snip, "They're so lucky," or whisper under their breath, "Those rich jerks."

You have to realize that if you view rich people as *bad* in any way, shape, or form, and you want to be a *good* person, then you can never be rich. It's impossible. How can you be something you despise?

It's amazing to witness the resentment and even outright anger that many poor people have toward the rich. As if they believe that rich people *make* them poor. "Yup, that's right, rich people took all the money so there's none left for me." Of course, this is perfect victim talk.

I want to tell you a story, not to complain, but simply to relate a real-world experience I had with this principle. In the old days, when I was, let's say, financially challenged, I used to drive a clunker. Changing lanes in traffic was never a problem. Almost everybody would let me in. But when I got rich and bought a gorgeous, new, black Jaguar, I couldn't help but notice how things changed. All of a sudden I started getting cut off and sometimes given the finger for added measure. I even got things thrown at me, all for one reason: I drove a Jag.

One day, I was driving through a lower-end neighborhood in San Diego, delivering turkeys for a charity at Christmastime. I had the sunroof open and I noticed four grimy guys perched in the back of a pickup truck behind me. Out of nowhere, they started playing basketball with my car, by attempting to shoot beer cans into my open sunroof. Five dents and several deep scratches later, they passed me screaming, "You rich bastard!"

Of course, I figured this to be an isolated incident, until just two weeks later, in a different lower-end neighborhood, I parked my car on the street and returned to it less than ten minutes later, to discover that the entire side of my car had been keyed.

The next time I went to that area of town, I rented a Ford Escort, and amazingly, I didn't have a single problem. I'm not implying that poorer neighborhoods have bad people, but in my experience, they sure seem to have plenty of folks who resent the rich. Who knows, maybe it's some kind of chicken-and-egg thing: Is it because they're broke that they resent the rich, or because they resent rich people that they're broke. As far as I'm concerned, who cares? It's all the same, they're still poor!

It's easy to talk about not resenting the rich, but depending on your mood, falling into the trap can happen to anyone, even me. Recently, I was eating dinner in my hotel room, about an hour before going onstage to teach an evening session of the Millionaire Mind seminar. I turned on the tube to check the sports scores and found that *Oprah* was on. Although I'm not a big fan of television, I love Oprah. That woman has affected more people in a positive way than almost anyone else on the planet, and consequently she deserves every penny she's got . . . and more!

Meanwhile, she's interviewing actress Halle Berry. They're discussing how Halle has just received one of the largest film contracts in history for a female actor—$20 million. Halle then says that she doesn't care about the money, and that she fought for this humongous contract to blaze a trail for other women to follow. I heard myself say skeptically, "Yeah, right! Do you think I and everyone else watching this show is an idiot? You should take a hunk of that dough and give your public relations agent a raise. That's the best sound-bite writing I've ever heard."

I felt the negativity welling up inside me, and just in the nick of time I caught myself, before the energy took me over. "Cancel, cancel, thank you for sharing," I yelled out loud to my mind, to drown out that voice of resentment.

I couldn't believe it. Here I was, Mr. Millionaire Mind himself, actually resenting Halle Berry for the money she made. I quickly turned it around and began screaming at the top of my lungs, "Way to go, girl! You rock! You let 'em off too cheap, you should've got thirty million dollars! Good for you. You're incredible and you deserve it." I felt a lot better.

Regardless of her reason for wanting all that money, the problem wasn't her, it was me. Remember, my opinions make no difference to Halle's happiness or wealth, but they do make a difference to *my* happiness and wealth. Also remember that thoughts and opinions aren't good or bad, right or wrong, as they enter your mind, but they can sure be empowering or disempowering to your happiness and success, as they enter your life.

The moment I felt that negative energy run through me, my "observation" alarms went off, and as I've trained myself to do, I immediately *neutralized* the negativity in my mind. You don't have to be perfect to get rich, but you do need to recognize when your thinking isn't empowering to yourself or others, then quickly refocus on more supportive thoughts. The more you study this book, the faster and easier this process will be, and if you attend the Millionaire Mind Intensive Seminar, you will dramatically accelerate your progress. I know I keep mentioning the Millionaire Mind course, but please understand, I wouldn't be so adamant about this program if I didn't see for myself the phenomenal results people get in their lives.

In their outstanding book *The One Minute Millionaire,* my good friends Mark Victor Hansen and Robert Allen quote the poignant story of Russell H. Conwell in his book, *Acres of Diamonds,* which was written over a hundred years ago:

I say that you ought to get rich, and it is your duty to get rich. How many of my pious brethren say to me, "Do you, a Christian minister, spend your time going up and down the country advising young people to get rich, to get money?" Yes, of course I do.

They say, "Isn't that awful! Why don't you preach the gospel instead of preaching about man's making money?" Because to make money honestly is to preach the gospel. That is the reason. The men who get rich may be the most honest men you find in the community.

"Oh," but says some young man here tonight, "I have been told all my life that if a person has money he is very dishonest and dishonorable and mean and contemptible." My friend, that is the reason you have none, because you have that idea of people. The foundation of your faith is altogether false. Let me say clearly . . . ninety-eight out of one hundred of the rich men (and women) of America are honest. That is why they are rich. That is why they are trusted with money. That is why they carry on great enterprises and find plenty of people to work with them.

Says another young man, "I hear sometimes of men that get millions of dollars dishonestly." Yes, of course you do, and so do

I. But they are so rare a thing in fact that the newspapers talk about them all the time as a matter of news until you get the idea that all the other rich men got rich dishonestly.

My friend, you . . . drive me . . . out into the suburbs of Philadelphia, and introduce me to the people who own their homes around this great city, so beautiful homes with gardens and flowers, those magnificent homes so lovely in their art, and I will introduce you to the very best people in character as well as in enterprise in our city. . . . They that own their homes are made more honorable and honest and pure, and true and economical and careful, by owning them.

We preach against covetousness . . . in the pulpit . . . and use the terms . . . "filthy lucre" so extremely that Christians get the idea that . . . it is wicked for any man to have money. Money is power, and you ought to be reasonably ambitious to have it! You ought because you can do more good with it than you can without it. Money printed your Bibles, money builds your churches, money sends your missionaries, and money pays your preachers. . . . I say, then, you ought to have money. If you can honestly attain unto riches . . . it is your . . . godly duty to do so. It is an awful mistake of these pious people to think you must be awfully poor in order to be pious.

Conwell's passage makes several excellent points. The first refers to the ability to be *trusted*. Of all the attributes necessary for getting rich, having others trust you has to be near the top of the list. Think about it, would you do business with a person you didn't trust at least to some extent? No way! Meaning that to get rich, there's a good chance many, many, many people must trust you, and there's a good chance that for that many people to trust you, you have to be quite trustworthy.

What other traits does a person need to get rich and, even more importantly, stay rich? No doubt there are always exceptions to any rule, but for the most part, *who* do you have to be to succeed at anything? Try some of these characteristics on for size: positive, reliable, focused, determined, persistent, hardworking, energetic, good with people, a competent communicator, semi-intelligent, and an expert in at least one area.

Another interesting element in Conwell's passage is that so many people have been conditioned to believe that you can't be rich and a good person or rich and spiritual. I too used to think this way. Like many of us, I was told by friends, teachers, media, and the rest of society that rich people were somehow bad, that they were all greedy. Once again, another way of thinking that ended up being pure crapola! Backed by my own real-world experience, rather than old, fear-based myth, I have found that the richest people I know are also the nicest.

When I moved to San Diego, we moved into a home in one of the richest parts of town. We loved the beauty of the home and the area, but I had some trepidation because I didn't know anyone and felt I didn't yet fit in. My plan was to stay low-key and not mix much with these rich snobs. As the universe would have it, however, my kids, who were five and seven years old at the time, made friends with the other kids in the neighborhood, and pretty soon I was driving them to these mansions to drop them off to play. I remember knocking on a stunningly carved wooden door that was at least twenty feet high. The mom opened it up and, with the friendliest voice I'd ever heard, said, "Harv, it's so great to meet you, come on in." I was a bit bewildered as she poured me some iced tea and got me a bowl of fruit. "What's the catch?" my skeptical mind kept wanting to know. Then her husband came in from playing with his kids in the pool. He was even friendlier: "Harv, we're so happy to have you in the neighborhood. You have to come to our BBQ tonight with the rest of your family. We'll introduce you to everybody, and we're not taking no for an answer. By the way, do you golf? I'm playing tomorrow at the club, why don't you come as my guest." By now I was in shock. What happened to the snobs I was sure I was going to meet? I left and went back home to tell my wife we were going to the BBQ.

"Oh, my," she said, "what will I wear?" "No, honey, you don't understand," I said, "these people are incredibly nice and totally informal. Just be who you are."

We went and that evening met some of the warmest, kindest, most generous, most loving people of our lives. At one point the conversation shifted to a charity drive that one of the guests was heading up. One after another, the checkbooks came out. I couldn't believe it, I was actually watching a lineup to give this woman money. But each check came with a catch. The agreement was that there would be reciprocity and that the woman would support the charity the donor was involved in. That's right, to a T, every person there either headed up or was a major player in a charity.

Our friends who had invited us were involved in several. In fact, each year they made it their goal to be the single largest donor in the entire city to the Children's Hospital Fund. They not only gave tens of thousands of dollars themselves, but every year they organized a dinner gala that raised hundreds of thousands more.

Then there was the "vein" doctor. We became quite close with his family too. He was among the top varicose vein doctors in the world and made a fortune; somewhere in the range of $5,000 to $10,000 per surgery, doing four or five surgeries per day.

I bring him up because every Tuesday was "free" day, when he would do surgeries on people in the city who couldn't afford to pay. On this day, he would work from 6:00 a.m. to 10:00 p.m. doing as many as ten surgeries, all for free. On top of this, he headed up his own organization whose mission was to get other doctors to do free days for people in their communities too.

Needless to say, my old, conditioned belief that rich people were greedy snobs dissipated in the light of reality. Now I know the opposite to be true. In my experience, the richest people I know are the nicest people I know. They are also the most generous. Not to say that people who aren't rich aren't nice or generous. But I can safely say the idea that all rich people are somehow bad is nothing more than ignorance.

The fact is, resenting the rich is one of the surest ways to stay broke. We are creatures of habit, and to overcome this or any other habit, we need to practice. Instead of resenting rich people, I want you to practice *admiring* rich people, I want you to practice *blessing* rich people, and I want you to practice *loving* rich people. That way, unconsciously you know that when you become rich, other people will admire you, bless you, and love you instead of resent the heck out of you the way you might do them now.

One of the philosophies I live by comes from ancient Huna wisdom, the original teachings of the Hawaiian elders. It goes like this: bless that which you want. If you see a person with a beautiful home, bless that person and bless that home. If you see a person with a beautiful car, bless that person and bless that car. If you see a person with a loving family, bless that person and bless that family. If you see a person with a beautiful body, bless that person and bless their body.

WEALTH PRINCIPLE:
"Bless that which you want." —Huna philosophy

The point is, if you resent what people have, in any way, shape, or form, you can never have it.

Regardless: if you see a person in a gorgeous black Jaguar with the sunroof open, *don't throw beer cans at it!*

DECLARATIONS: Place your hand on your heart and say . . .

"I admire rich people!"
"I bless rich people!"
"I love rich people!"
"And I'm going to be one of those rich people too!"

Touch your head and say . . .

"I have a millionaire mind!"

MILLIONAIRE MIND ACTIONS

1. Practice the Huna philosophy "bless that which you want." Drive around or buy magazines, look at beautiful homes, gorgeous cars, and read about successful businesses. Whatever you see that you like, bless it, and bless the owners or the people involved.

2. Write and send a short letter or e-mail to someone you know of (not necessarily personally) who is highly successful in any arena, telling them how much you admire and honor them for their achievements.

Wealth File #7

Rich people associate with positive, successful people. Poor people associate with negative or unsuccessful people.

Successful people look at other successful people as a means to motivate themselves. They see other successful people as models to learn from. They say to themselves, "If they can do it, I can do it." As I mentioned earlier, modeling is one of the primary ways that people learn.

Rich people are grateful that others have succeeded before them so that they now have a blueprint to follow that will make it easier to attain their own success. Why reinvent the wheel? There are proven methods for success that work for virtually everyone who applies them.

Consequently, the fastest and easiest way to create wealth is to learn exactly how rich people, who are masters of money, play the game. The goal is to simply model their inner and outer strategies. It just makes sense: if you take the exact same actions and have the exact same mind-set, chances are good you will get the exact same results. That's what I did and that's what this entire book is about.

Contrary to the rich, when poor people hear about other people's success, they often judge them, criticize them, mock them, and try to pull them down to their own level. How many of you know people like this? How many of you know family members like this? The question is, how can you possibly learn from or be inspired by someone you put down?

Whenever I'm introduced to an extremely rich person, I create a way to get together with them. I want to talk to them, learn how they think, exchange contacts, and if we have other things in common, possibly become personal friends with them.

By the way, if you think I'm wrong for preferring to be friends with rich people, perhaps you'd rather I pick friends who are broke? I don't think so! As I've mentioned before, energy is contagious, and I have no interest in subjecting myself to theirs!

I was recently doing a radio interview and a woman called in with an excellent question: "What do I do if I'm positive and want to grow, but my husband is a downer? Do I leave him? Do I try and get him to change? What?" I hear this question at least a hundred times a week when I'm teaching our courses. Almost everyone asks the same question: "What if the people I'm closest to aren't into personal growth and even put me down for it?"

Here's the answer I gave the woman on the call, what I tell people at our courses, and what I'm suggesting to you.

First, don't bother trying to get negative people to change or come to the course. That's not your job. Your job is to use what you've learned to better yourself and your life. Be the model, be successful, be happy, then maybe—and I stress *maybe*—they'll see the light (in you) and want some of it. Again, energy is contagious. Darkness dissipates in light. People actually have to work hard to stay "dark" when light is all around them. Your job is simply to be the best you can be. If they choose to ask you your secret, tell them.

Second, keep in mind another principle that we feature in our Wizard Training, which is a course about manifesting what you want while staying calm, centered, and peaceful. It states, "Everything happens for a reason and that reason is there to assist me." Yes, it's much more difficult to be positive and conscious around people and circumstances that are negative, but that's your test! Just as steel is hardened in the fire, if you can remain true to your values while others around you are full of doubt and even condemnation, you'll grow faster and stronger.

Also remember that "nothing has meaning except for the meaning we give it." Recall in Part I of this book, we discussed how we usually end up identifying with or rebelling against one or both of our parents, depending on how we "framed" their actions. From now on, I want you to practice reframing other people's negativity as a reminder of how *not* to be. The more negative they are, the more reminders you have about how *ugly* that way of being really is. I'm not suggesting you tell them this. Just do it, without condemning them for how they are. For if you do begin to judge, criticize, and put them down for who they are and what they do, then you are no better than them.

Worse comes to worst, if you just can't handle their non-supportive energy anymore, if it's bringing you down to a point where you're not able to grow, you may have to make some courageous decisions about who you are and how you want to live the rest of your life. I'm not suggesting you do anything rash, but I for one would never live with a person who was negative and pooh-poohed my desire to learn and grow, be it personally, spiritually, or financially. I wouldn't do that to myself because I respect myself and my life and I deserve to be as happy and successful as possible. The way I figure it, there are over 6.3 billion people in the world and there's no way I'm going to saddle myself with a downer. Either they move up or I move on!

Again, energy is contagious: either you *affect* people or

infect people. The same holds true the opposite way around; either people affect or infect you. Let me ask you a question: Would you hug and hold a person you knew had a severe case of the measles? Most people would say, "No way, I don't want to catch the measles." Well, I believe negative thinking is like having *measles of the mind.* Instead of itching, you get bitching; instead of scratching, you get bashing; instead of irritation, you get frustration. Now, do you really want to be close to people like that?

I'm sure you've heard the saying "Birds of a feather flock together." Did you know that most people earn within 20 percent of the average income of their closest friends? That's why you'd better watch whom you associate with and choose whom you spend your time with carefully.

From my experience, rich people don't just join the country club to play golf; they join to connect with other rich and successful people. There's another saying that goes "It's not what you know, it's *who* you know." As far as I'm concerned, you can take that to the bank. In short, "If you want to fly with the eagles, don't swim with the ducks!" I make it a point to only associate with successful, positive people, and just as importantly, I disassociate from negative ones.

I also make it a point to remove myself from toxic situations. I see no reason for infecting myself with poisonous energy. Among these I would include arguing, gossiping, and backstabbing. I would also include watching "mindless" television, unless you use it specifically as a relaxation strategy instead of your sole form of entertainment. When I watch TV, it's usually sports. First, because I enjoy seeing masters at anything at work or in this case play, and second because I enjoy listening to the interviews after the games. I love listening to the mind-set of champions, and to me, anyone who has made it as far as the big leagues in any sport is a champion. Any athlete at that level has outcompeted tens of thousands of other players to get there at all, which makes each of them incredible to me. I love hearing their attitude when they win: "It was a great effort from the entire team. We did well but we still have improvements to make. It goes to show you that hard work pays off." I also love listening to their attitude when they lose: "It's only one game. We'll be back, we're just going to forget about this one and put our focus on the next game. We'll go back and talk about where we can do better, and then do whatever it takes to win."

During the 2004 Olympic Games, Perdita Felicien, a Canadian and the reigning world champion in the hundred-meter hurdles, was heavily favored to win the gold medal. In the final race, she hit the first hurdle and fell hard. She wasn't able to complete the race. Extremely upset, she had tears in her eyes as she lay there in bewilderment. She had prepared for this moment six hours a day, every day of the week, for the past four years. The next morning, I saw her news conference. I wish I had taped it. It was amazing to listen to her perspective. She said something to the effect of "I don't know why it happened but it did, and I'm going to use it. I'm going to focus even more and work even harder for the next four years. Who knows what my path would have been had I won? Maybe it would have dulled my desire. I don't know, but I do know that now I'm hungrier than ever. I'll be back even stronger." As I heard her speak, all I could say was "Wow!" You can learn a lot from listening to champions.

Rich people hang around with winners. Poor people hang around with losers. Why? It's a matter of comfort. Rich people are comfortable with other successful people. They feel fully worthy of being with them. Poor people are uncomfortable with highly successful people. They're either afraid they'll be rejected or feel as if they don't belong. To protect itself, the ego then goes into judgment and criticism.

If you want to get rich, you will have to change your inner blueprint to fully believe you are every bit as good as any millionaire or multimillionaire out there. I'm shocked in my seminars when people come up to me and ask if they can touch me. They say, "I've never touched a multimillionaire before." I'm usually polite and smile, but in my mind I'm saying, "Get a frickin' life! I'm no better or different from you, and unless you start to understand that, you'll stay broke forever!"

My friends, it's not about "touching" millionaires, it's about deciding that you are just as good and worthy as they are, and then acting like it. My best advice is this: if you really want to touch a millionaire, become one!

I hope you get the point. Instead of mocking rich people, model them. Instead of shying away from rich people, get to know them. Instead of saying, "Wow, they're so special," say, "If they can do it, I can do it." Eventually, if you want to touch a millionaire, you'll be able to touch yourself!

DECLARATIONS: Place your hand on your heart and say . . .

> *"I model rich and successful people."*
> *"I associate with rich and successful people."*
> *"If they can do it, I can do it!"*

Touch your head and say . . .

> *"I have a millionaire mind!"*

MILLIONAIRE MIND ACTIONS

1. Go to the library, a bookstore, or the Internet and read a biography of someone who is or was extremely rich and successful. Andrew Carnegie, John D. Rockefeller, Mary Kay, Donald Trump, Warren Buffett, Jack Welch, Bill Gates, and Ted Turner are some good examples. Use their story for inspiration, for learning specific success strategies, and most importantly, for copying their mind-set.

2. Join a high-end club, such as for tennis, health, business, or golf. Mingle with rich people in a rich environment. Or, if there's no way you can afford to join a high-end club, have coffee or tea in the classiest hotel in your city. Get comfortable in this atmosphere and watch the patrons, noticing they're no different from you.

3. Identify a situation or a person who is a downer in your life. Remove yourself from that situation or association. If it's family, choose to be around them less.

4. Stop watching trash TV and stay away from bad news.

Wealth File #8

Rich people are willing to promote themselves and their value. Poor people think negatively about selling and promotion.

My company, Peak Potentials Training, offers over a dozen different programs. During the initial seminar, usually the

Millionaire Mind Intensive, we briefly mention a few of our other courses, then offer the participants special "at seminar" tuition rates and bonuses. It's interesting to note the reactions.

Most people are thrilled. They appreciate getting to hear what the other courses are about and to receive the special pricing. Some people, however, are not so thrilled. They resent any promotion regardless of how it might benefit them. If this sounds in any way like you, it's an important characteristic to notice about yourself.

Resenting promotion is one of the greatest obstacles to success. People who have issues with selling and promotion are usually broke. It's obvious. How can you create a large income in your own business or as a representative of one if you aren't willing to let people know that you, your product, or your service exists? Even as an employee, if you aren't willing to promote your virtues, someone who is willing will quickly bypass you on the corporate ladder.

People have a problem with promotion or sales for several reasons. Chances are you might recognize one or more of the following.

First, you may have had a bad experience in the past with people promoting to you inappropriately. Maybe you perceived they were doing the "hard" sell on you. Maybe they were bothering you at an inopportune time. Maybe they wouldn't take no for an answer. In any case, it's important to recognize that this experience is in the past and that holding on to it may not be serving you today.

Second, you may have had a disempowering experience when you tried to sell something to someone and that person totally rejected you. In this instance, your distaste for promotion is merely a projection of your own fear of failure and rejection. Again, realize the past does not necessarily equal the future.

Third, your issue might come from past parental programming. Many of us were told that it's impolite to "toot your own horn." Well, that's great if you make a living as Miss Manners. But in the real world, when it comes to business and money, if you don't toot your horn, I guarantee nobody will. Rich people are willing to extol their virtues and value to anyone who will listen and hopefully do business with them as well.

Finally, some people feel that promotion is *beneath* them. I call this the high-and-mighty syndrome, otherwise known as the "Aren't I so special?" attitude. The feeling in this case is that if people want what you have, they should somehow find and come to you. People who have this belief are either broke or soon will be, that's for sure. They can hope that everyone's going to scour the land searching for them, but the truth is that the marketplace is crowded with products and services, and even though theirs may be the best, no one will ever know that because they're too snooty to tell anyone.

You're probably familiar with the saying "Build a better mousetrap and the world will beat a path to your door." Well, that's only true if you add five words: "if they know about it."

Rich people are almost always excellent promoters. They can and are willing to promote their products, their services, and their ideas with passion and enthusiasm. What's more, they're skilled at packaging their value in a way that's extremely attractive. If you think there's something wrong with that, then let's ban makeup for women, and while we're at it, we might as well get rid of suits for men. All that is nothing more than "packaging."

Robert Kiyosaki, best-selling author of *Rich Dad, Poor Dad* (a book I highly recommend), points out that every business, including writing books, depends on selling. He notes that he is recognized as a best-*selling* author, not a best-*writing* author. One pays a lot more than the other.

Rich people are usually leaders, and all great leaders are great promoters. To be a leader, you must inherently have followers and supporters, which means that you have to be adept at selling, inspiring, and motivating people to buy into your vision. Even the president of the United States of America has to continuously sell his ideas to the people, to Congress, and even to his own party, to have them implemented. And way before all of that takes place, if he doesn't sell *himself* in the first place, he'll never even get elected.

In short, any leader who can't or won't promote will not be a leader for long, be it in politics, business, sports, or even as a parent. I'm harping on this because *leaders earn a heck of a lot more money than followers*!

WEALTH PRINCIPLE:
Leaders earn a heck of a lot more money
than followers!

The critical point here isn't whether you like to promote or not, it is *why* you're promoting. It boils down to your beliefs. Do you really believe in your value? Do you really believe in the product or service you're offering? Do you really believe that what you have will be of benefit to whomever you're promoting it to?

If you believe in your value, how could it possibly be appropriate to hide it from people who need it? Suppose you had a cure for arthritis, and you met someone who was suffering and in pain with the disease. Would you hide it from him or her? Would you wait for that person to read your mind or guess that you have a product that could help? What would you think of someone who didn't offer suffering people their opportunity because they were too shy, too afraid, or too cool to promote?

More often than not, people who have a problem with promotion don't fully believe in their product or don't fully believe in themselves. Consequently, it's difficult for them to imagine that other people believe so strongly in their value that they want to share it with everyone who comes their way and in any way they can.

If you believe that what you have to offer can truly assist people, it's your duty to let as many people as possible know about it. In this way, you not only help people, you get rich!

DECLARATION: Place your hand on your heart and say . . .

"I promote my value to others with passion and enthusiasm."

Touch your head and say . . .

"I have a millionaire mind!"

MILLIONAIRE MIND ACTIONS

1. Rate the product or service you are currently offering (or you are planning to offer) from 1 to 10 in terms of how much you believe in its value (1 being the lowest, 10 being the highest). If your rating result is 7–9,

revise your product or service to increase the value. If your result is 6 or below, stop offering that product or service and start representing something you truly believe in.

2. Read books, listen to audios and CDs, and take courses on marketing and sales. Become an expert in both of these arenas to a point where you can promote your value successfully and with 100 percent integrity.

Wealth File #9

Rich people are bigger than their problems.
Poor people are smaller than their problems.

As I said earlier, getting rich is not a stroll in the park. It is a journey that is full of twists, turns, detours, and obstacles. The road to wealth is fraught with traps and pitfalls, and that's precisely why most people don't take it. They don't want the hassles, the headaches, and the responsibilities. In short, they don't want the problems.

Therein lies one of the biggest differences between rich people and poor people. Rich and successful people are bigger than their problems, while poor and unsuccessful people are smaller than their problems.

Poor people will do almost anything to avoid problems. They see a challenge and they run. The irony is that in their quest to make sure they don't have problems, they have the biggest problem of all . . . they're broke and miserable. The secret to success, my friends, is not to try to avoid or get rid of or shrink from your problems; the secret is to grow yourself so that you are bigger than any problem.

WEALTH PRINCIPLE:
The secret to success is not to try to avoid
or get rid of or shrink from your problems;
the secret is to grow yourself so that
you are bigger than any problem.

On a scale of 1 to 10, 1 being the lowest, imagine you are a person with a level 2 strength of character and attitude looking at a level 5 problem. Would this problem appear to be big or little? From a level 2 perspective, a level 5 problem would seem like a *big* problem.

Now imagine you've grown yourself and become a level 8 person. Would the same level 5 problem be a big problem or a little problem? Magically, the identical problem is now a little problem.

Finally, imagine you've really worked hard on yourself and become a level 10 person. Now, is this same level 5 problem a big problem or a little problem? The answer is that it's *no* problem. It doesn't even register in your brain as a problem. There's no negative energy around it. It's just a normal occurrence to handle, like brushing your teeth or getting dressed.

Note that whether you are rich or poor, playing big or playing small, problems do not go away. If you're breathing, you will always have so-called problems and obstacles in your life. Let me make this short and sweet. The size of the problem is never the issue—what matters is the size of you!

This may be painful, but if you're ready to move to the next level of success, you're going to have to become conscious of what's really going on in your life. Ready? Here goes.

If you have a big problem in your life, all that means is that you are being a small person! Don't be fooled by appearances. Your outer world is merely a reflection of your inner world. If you want to make a permanent change, stop focusing on the size of your problems and start focusing on the size of you!

WEALTH PRINCIPLE:
If you have a big problem in your life, all that means is that you are being a small person!

One of the not-so-subtle reminders I give participants at my seminar is this: whenever you feel as if you've got a big problem, point to yourself and scream, "Mini me, mini me, mini me!" That will abruptly wake you up and move your attention back to where it belongs—on yourself. Then, coming from your "higher self" (rather than your ego-based, victim self), take a deep breath and decide right now, in this very moment, you will be a bigger person and not allow any problem or obstacle to take you out of either your happiness or success.

The bigger the problems you can handle, the bigger the business you can handle; the bigger the responsibility you can handle, the more employees you can handle; the more customers you can handle, the more money you can handle, and ultimately, the more wealth you can handle.

Again, your wealth can only grow to the extent that you do! The objective is to grow yourself to a place where you can overcome any problems or obstacles that get in the way of your creating wealth and keeping it once you have it.

By the way, *keeping* your wealth is a whole other world.

Who knew? I sure didn't. I thought that once you made it, you made it! Boy, was I in for a rude awakening as I proceeded to lose my first million almost as fast as I made it. Now, in hindsight, I understand what the issue was. At the time, my "toolbox" wasn't yet big and strong enough to hold the wealth I had achieved. Again, thank goodness I practiced the principles of the Millionaire Mind and was able to recondition myself! Not only did I make that million back, but because of my new "money blueprint," I've made millions and millions more. Best of all, I've not only kept it, but it keeps *growing* at a phenomenal rate!

Think of yourself as your container for wealth. If your container is small and your money is big, what's going to happen? You will lose it. Your container will overflow and the excess money will spill out all over the place. You simply cannot have more money than the container. Therefore you must grow to be a big container so you cannot only *hold* more wealth but also *attract* more wealth. The universe abhors a vacuum and if you have a very large money container, it will rush in to fill the space.

One of the reasons rich people are bigger than their problems goes back to what we discussed earlier. They don't focus on the problem; they focus on their goal. Again, the mind generally focuses on one predominant thing at a time. Meaning that either you are whining about the problem or you are working on the solution. Rich and successful people are solution-oriented; they spend their time and energy strategizing and planning the answers to challenges that come up, and creating systems to make certain that problem doesn't occur again.

Poor and unsuccessful people are problem-oriented. They spend their time and energy bitching and complaining and seldom come up with anything creative to alleviate the problem, let alone make sure it doesn't happen again.

Rich people do not back away from problems, do not avoid problems, and do not complain about problems. Rich people are financial warriors. In our Enlightened Warrior Training Camp, the definition of a warrior we use is "one who conquers oneself."

The bottom line is that if you become a master at handling problems and overcoming any obstacle, what can stop you from success? The answer is *nothing*! And if nothing can stop you, you become *unstoppable*! And if you become unstoppable, what choices do you have in your life? The answer is *all* choices. If you are unstoppable, anything and everything is available to you. You simply choose it and it's yours! How's that for freedom!

DECLARATIONS: Place your hand on your heart and say . . .

"I am bigger than any problems."
"I can handle any problems."

Touch your head and say . . .

"I have a millionaire mind!"

MILLIONAIRE MIND ACTIONS

1. Whenever you are feeling upset over a "big" problem, point to yourself and say, "Mini me, mini me." Then take a deep breath and say to yourself, "I can handle this. I am bigger than any problem."

2. Write down a problem you are having in your life. Then list ten specific actions you can take to resolve or at least improve this situation. This will move you

from problem thinking into solution thinking. First, there's a good chance you'll solve the problem. Second, you'll feel a heck of a lot better.

Wealth File #10

Rich people are excellent receivers.
Poor people are poor receivers.

If I had to nail down the number one reason most people do not reach their full financial potential, it would be this: most people are poor "receivers." They may or may not be good at giving, but they are definitely bad at receiving. And because they are poor at receiving, they don't!

People are challenged by receiving for several reasons. First, many people feel unworthy or undeserving. This syndrome runs rampant in our society. I would guess that over 90 percent of individuals have feelings of not being good enough running through their veins.

Where does this low self-esteem come from? The usual—our conditioning. For most of us it comes from hearing twenty nos for every yes, ten "You're doing it wrong"s for every "You're doing it right," and five "You're stupid"s for every "You're awesome."

Even if our parents or guardians were incredibly supportive, many of us end up with feelings of not being able to continually measure up to their accolades and expectations. So once again, we're not good enough.

In addition, most of us grew up with the element of punishment in our lives. This unwritten rule simply states that if you do something wrong, you will or should be punished. Some of us were punished by our parents, some by our teachers . . . and some of us in certain religious circles were threatened with the mother of all punishments, not getting into heaven.

Of course, now that we're adults, all this is over. Right? Wrong! For most people, the conditioning of punishment is so ingrained that, because there's no one around to punish them, when they make a mistake or just aren't perfect, they subconsciously punish themselves. When they were young, this punishment might have come in the form of "You were bad, so no candy." Today, however, it could take the form of "You were bad, so no money." This explains why some people limit their earnings, and why others will subconsciously sabotage their success.

No wonder people have difficulty receiving. One tiny mistake and you're doomed to carry the burden of misery and poverty for the rest of your life. "A little harsh," you say? Since when did the mind become logical or compassionate? Again, the conditioned mind is a file folder filled with past programming, made-up meanings, and stories of drama and disaster. "Making sense" is not its strong suit.

Here's something I teach in my seminars that might make you feel better. In the end, it doesn't matter whether you feel worthy or not, you can be rich either way. Plenty of wealthy people don't feel overly worthy. In fact, it's one of the major motivations for people to get rich . . . to *prove* themselves and their worth to themselves or to others. The idea that self-worth is necessary for net worth is just that, an idea, but it doesn't necessarily hold water in the real world. As we said earlier, getting rich to prove yourself may not make you the happiest camper, so you're better off creating wealth for other reasons. But what's important here is for you to realize that your feeling of unworthiness won't prevent you from getting rich; from a strictly financial point of view this could actually be a motivational asset.

Having said that, I want you to get what I'm going to share with you, loud and clear. This could easily be one of the most important moments of your life. Are you ready? Here goes.

Recognize that whether you are worthy or not is all a made-up "story." Again, nothing has meaning except for the meaning we give it. I don't know about you, but I've never heard of anybody who went through the "stamping" lineup at birth. Can you imagine God stamping each person's forehead as he or she came through? "Worthy . . . unworthy . . . worthy, worthy . . . unworthy. Yuck . . . definitely unworthy." Sorry, I don't think it works that way. There's no one who comes around and stamps you "worthy" or "unworthy." You do that. You make it up. You decide it. You and you alone determine if you're going to be worthy. It's simply your perspective. If you say you're worthy, you are. If you say you're not worthy, you're not. Either way you will live into your story. This is so critical, I'm going to repeat that again: you will live into your story. It's that simple.

WEALTH PRINCIPLE:
If you say you're worthy, you are.
If you say you're not worthy, you're not.
Either way you will live into your story.

So why would people do this to themselves? Why would people make up the story that they're not worthy? It's just the nature of the human mind, the protective part of us that's always looking for what's wrong. Ever notice that a squirrel doesn't worry about these things? Can you imagine a squirrel saying, "I'm not going to collect many nuts this year to prepare for winter because I'm not worthy?" Doubtful, because these low-intelligence creatures would never do that to themselves. Only the most evolved creature on the planet, the human being, has the ability to limit itself like this.

One of my own sayings is "If a hundred-foot oak tree had the mind of a human, it would only grow to be ten feet tall!" So here's my suggestion: since it's a lot easier to change your story than your worthiness, instead of worrying about changing your worthiness, change your story. It's a lot faster and cheaper. Simply make up a new and much more supportive story and live into that.

"Oh, but I couldn't do that," you say. "I'm not qualified to decide that I'm worthy. That has to come from someone else." Sorry, I say, that's not quite accurate, which is a nice way of saying "Bullpoo!" It wouldn't make a difference what anyone says or said in the past, because you have to believe it and buy into it for it to have any effect and that can't come from anyone else but you. But just to make you feel better, let's play the game and I'll do for you what I do for thousands of participants at the Millionaire Mind Intensive Seminar: I will personally anoint you.

WEALTH PRINCIPLE:
"If a hundred-foot oak tree had the mind of a human, it would only grow to be ten feet tall!"
—T. Harv Eker

This is a special ceremony, so I'm going to ask you to eliminate any distractions right now. Stop munching, stop talking on the phone, and stop whatever you're doing. Men, if you like, you can change into a suit and tie, although a tuxedo would be best. Women, a formal evening gown and heels would be perfect. And if you don't have anything that's classy or new enough, this would definitely be an occasion to go buy yourself a brand-new dress, designer label preferred.

If you're all ready, let's begin. Please kneel down on one knee and bow your head in respect. Ready, here goes. "BY THE POWER INVESTED IN ME, I HEREBY ANOINT YOU AS 'WORTHY' FROM NOW UNTIL FOREVER MORE!"

Okay we're done. You can stand up now and hold your head high because you are finally worthy. Here's some sage advice: stop buying into that "worthiness" or "unworthiness" crap and start taking the actions you need to take to get rich!

The second major reason most people have a problem with receiving is that they have bought into the adage "It's better to give than to receive." Let me put this as elegantly as possible: "What a *crock*!" That statement is total hogwash, and in case you haven't noticed, it's usually propagated by people and groups who want you to give and them to receive.

The whole idea is ludicrous. What's better, hot or cold, big or small, left or right, in or out? Giving and receiving are two sides of the same coin. Whoever decided that it is better to give than to receive was simply bad at math. For every giver there must be a receiver, and for every receiver there must be a giver.

WEALTH PRINCIPLE:
For every giver there must be a receiver,
and for every receiver there must be a giver.

Think about it! How could you give if there weren't someone or something there to receive? Both have to be in perfect balance to work one to one, fifty-fifty. And since giving and receiving must always equal each other, they must also be equal in importance.

Besides, how does it feel to give? Most of us would agree that giving feels wonderful and fulfilling. Conversely, how does it feel when you want to give and the other person isn't willing to receive? Most of us would agree that it feels terrible. So know this: *if you are not willing to receive, then you are "ripping off" those who want to give to you.*

You are actually denying them the joy and pleasure that comes from giving; instead, they feel lousy. Why? Again, everything is energy, and when you want to give but can't, that energy cannot be expressed and gets stuck in you. That "stuck" energy then turns into negative emotions.

To make matters worse, when you are not willing to fully receive, you are training the universe not to give to you! It's simple: if you aren't willing to receive your share, it will go to someone else who is. That's one of the reasons the rich get richer and the poor get poorer. Not because they're any more worthy, but because they are willing to receive while most poor people are not.

I learned this lesson in a big way while camping by myself in the forest. In preparation for my two-day sojourn I made what's called a lean-to. This means tying the top part of a tarp to a tree and then fastening the bottom to the ground to create a forty-five-degree roof over my head when I slept. Thank goodness I prepared this mini-condo because it rained all night. When I came out of my shelter that morning, I was noticing how dry I and everything else under the tarp was. At the same time, however, I couldn't help but notice this unusually deep puddle that had collected at the bottom of the tarp. All of a sudden I heard this inner voice say to me, "Nature is totally abundant but not discriminating. When the rain falls, it has to go somewhere. If one part is dry, another part will be doubly wet." As I stood over the puddle, I realized this is exactly the way it works with money. There's plenty of it, trillions of trillions of dollars floating around, it's in definite abundance, and it has to go somewhere. The deal is this: if somebody isn't willing to receive his or her share, it must go to whoever will. The rain doesn't care who gets it and neither does money.

At this point in the Millionaire Mind seminar I teach people the special prayer I created after my experience under the tarp. Of course it's a little tongue-in-cheek, but the lesson is obvious. It goes like this: "Universe, if anyone has something great coming to them and they're not willing to take it, send it to me! I am open and willing to receive all of your blessings. Thank you." I have the entire audience repeat this with me and they go crazy! They're excited because it feels amazing to be totally willing to receive, and it feels great because it's totally natural to do so. Anything you've made up to the contrary is, again, just a "story" that isn't serving you or anyone else. Let your story go and your money come.

Rich people work hard and believe it's perfectly appropriate to be well rewarded for their efforts and the value they provide for others. Poor people work hard, but due to their feelings of unworthiness, they believe that it is inappropriate for them to be well rewarded for their efforts and the value they provide. This belief sets them up to be perfect victims, and of course, how can you be a "good" victim if you are well rewarded?

Many poor people actually believe they are better people because they are poor. Somehow they believe they're more pious or spiritual or good. Baloney! The only thing poor people are, is poor. I had a gentleman at the course come to me in tears. He said, "I just don't see how I could feel good about having a lot of money when others have so little." I asked him a few simple questions: "What good do you do for poor people by being one of them? Whom do you help by being broke? Aren't you just another mouth to feed? Wouldn't it be more effective for you to create wealth for yourself and then be able to really help others from a place of strength instead of weakness?"

He stopped crying and said, "For the first time, I got it. I can't believe what garbage I've been thinking. Harv, I believe the time has come for me to get rich and, along the way, help others. Thank you." He went back to his seat a new man. I got an e-mail from him not long ago telling me he's making ten times what he used to earn and that he's feeling awesome about it. Best of all, he says, it feels tremendous to be able to assist some of his friends and family who are still struggling.

This leads me to an important point: if you have the wherewithal to have a lot of money, have it. Why? Because the truth is that we are extremely fortunate to be living in this society, a society whereby each person is in fact rich compared to many other parts of the world. Some people just don't ever have the opportunity to have a lot of money. If you are one of the lucky people who do have that ability, and each of you is or you wouldn't be reading a book like this, then use your wherewithal for all it's worth. Get really rich and then help people who don't have the opportunity you did. That makes a lot more sense to me than being broke and helping no one.

Of course there are the people who will say, "Money will change me. If I get rich, I might turn into some kind of greedy jerk." First, the only people who say that are poor people. It's just another justification for their failure, and it comes from just another one of the many "inner" weeds in their financial garden. Don't buy it!

Second, let me set the record straight. *Money will only make you more of what you already are.* If you're mean, money will afford you the opportunity to be meaner. If you're kind, money will afford you the opportunity to be kinder. If you're a jerk at heart, with money you can be jerkier. (I know there's no such word, but if you were a real jerk, you'd find a way.) If you're generous, more money will simply allow you to be more generous. And anyone who tells you different is *broke*!

WEALTH PRINCIPLE:
Money will only make you
more of what you already are.

So what to do? How do you become a good receiver?

First, begin to nurture yourself. Remember, people are creatures of habit, and therefore you will have to consciously practice receiving the best life has to offer.

One of the key elements in the money management system we teach in the Millionaire Mind Intensive Seminar is having a "play" account where you get to blow a designated amount of money on things that nurture you and allow you to "feel like a million." The idea of this account is to help you validate your worthiness and strengthen your "receiving muscle."

Second, I want you to practice going crazy with excitement and gratitude anytime you find or receive any money. It's funny, when I was broke and I saw a penny on the ground, I would never stoop so low as to pick up a lowly penny. Now that I'm rich, however, I pick up anything that even looks like money. Then I give it a kiss for good luck and declare out loud, "I am a money magnet. Thank you, thank you, thank you."

I don't stand there judging the denomination. Money is money, and finding money is a blessing from the universe. Now that I'm fully willing to receive anything and everything that comes my way, I do!

Being open and willing to receive is absolutely critical if you want to create wealth. It's also critical if you want to keep it. If you are a poor receiver and you somehow fall into a substantial amount of money, chances are it'll be gone quickly. Again, "first the inner, then the outer." First, expand your receiving "box." Then watch as the money comes in to fill it.

Again, the universe abhors a vacuum. In other words, an empty space will always be filled. Have you ever noticed what happens with an empty closet or garage? It usually doesn't stay empty for long, does it? Have you also noticed how strange it is that the time taken for any task will always be equal to the time given? Once you expand your capacity to receive, you will.

Also, once you become truly open to receiving, the rest of your life will open up. Not only will you receive more money, but you'll also receive more love, more peace, more happiness, and more fulfillment. Why? Because of another principle I constantly use that states, "How you do anything is how you do everything."

WEALTH PRINCIPLE:
How you do anything is how you do everything.

The way you are in one area is usually the way you are in all areas. If you've been blocking yourself from receiving money, chances are you've been blocking yourself from receiving everything else that's good in life. The mind doesn't usually delineate specifically where you are a poor receiver. In fact, it's just the opposite: the mind has a habit of over-generalizing and says, "The way it is, is the way it is, everywhere and always."

If you're a poor receiver, you're a poor receiver in all areas. The good news is that when you become an excellent receiver, you'll be an excellent receiver everywhere . . . and open to receiving *all* that the universe has to offer in *all* areas of your life.

Now the only thing you'll have to remember is to keep saying "Thank you" as you receive all of your blessings.

DECLARATION: Place your hand on your heart and say . . .

> *"I am an excellent receiver. I am open and willing to receive massive amounts of money into my life."*

Touch your head and say . . .

> *"I have a millionaire mind!"*

MILLIONAIRE MIND ACTIONS

1. Practice being an excellent receiver. Each time someone gives you a compliment of any sort, simply say,
   "Thank you." Do not return a compliment to that
   person at the same time. This allows you to fully receive and own the compliment instead of "deflecting"
   it, as most people do. This also allows the giver of the
   compliment the joy of giving the gift without it being
   thrown back at them.

2. Any, and I mean *any*, money you find or receive
   should enthusiastically be celebrated. Go ahead and
   scream out, "I'm a money magnet. Thank you, thank
   you, thank you." This goes for money you find on the
   ground, for money you get as gifts, for money you get
   from the government, for money you get as a paycheck, and for money you get from your business.
   Remember, the universe is set up to support you. If
   you keep declaring that you are a money magnet, and
   especially if you have the proof, the universe will
   simply say, "Okay," and send you more.

3. Pamper yourself. At least once a month do something
   special to nurture yourself and your spirit. Get a massage, a manicure, or a pedicure, take yourself for an
   extravagant lunch or dinner, rent a boat or a weekend
   cottage, have someone bring you breakfast in bed.
   (You might have to trade with a friend or family member.) Do things that will allow you to feel rich and de-
   serving. Again, the vibrational energy you emit from
   this kind of experience will send a message to the universe that you live abundantly, and again, the universe

will simply do its job and say, "Okay," and give you opportunities for more.

Wealth File #11

**Rich people choose to get paid based on results.
Poor people choose to get paid based on time.**

Have you ever heard this advice: "Go to school, get good grades, get a good job, get a steady paycheck, be on time, work hard . . . and you'll live happily ever after"? I don't know about you, but I'd sure love to see the written guarantee on that one. Unfortunately, this sage advice comes directly from the *Book of Fairy Tales, Volume I,* right after the tooth fairy story.

I'm not going to bother debunking the entire statement. You can do that for yourself by checking your own experience and the lives of everyone around you. What I will discuss is the idea behind the "steady" paycheck. There's nothing wrong with getting a steady paycheck, unless it interferes with your ability to earn what you're worth. There's the rub. It usually does.

WEALTH PRINCIPLE:
There's nothing wrong with getting a steady paycheck, unless it interferes with your ability to earn what you're worth. There's the rub. It usually does.

Poor people prefer to be paid a steady salary or hourly wage. They need the "security" of knowing that exactly the same amount of money is coming in at exactly the same time, month in, month out. What they don't realize is that this security comes with a price, and the cost is wealth.

Living based in security is living based in fear. What you're actually saying is "I'm afraid I won't be able to earn enough based on my performance, so I'll settle for earning just enough to survive or to be comfortable."

Rich people prefer to get paid based on the results they produce, if not totally, then at least partially. Rich people usually own their own business in some form. They make their income from their profits. Rich people work on commission or percentages of revenue. Rich people choose stock options and profit sharing in lieu of higher salaries. Notice there are no guarantees with any of the above. As stated earlier, in the financial world the rewards are usually proportionate to the risk.

Rich people believe in themselves. They believe in their value and in their ability to deliver it. Poor people don't. That's why they need "guarantees."

Recently, I dealt with a public relations consultant who wanted me to pay her a fee of $4,000 per month. I asked her what I'd receive for my $4,000. She replied that I'd see at least $20,000 of coverage per month in the media. I said, "What if you don't produce those results or anything close to it?" She answered that she would still be putting in the time, so she deserved to get paid.

I replied, "I'm not interested in paying for your time. I'm interested in paying you for a specific result, and if you don't produce that result, why should I pay you? On the other hand, if you produce even greater results, you should get paid more. Tell you what: I'll give you fifty percent of whatever media value you produce. According to your figures, that would mean paying you ten thousand dollars per month, which is more than double your fee."

Did she go for it? Nope! Is she broke? Yup! And she will be for the rest of her life or until she figures out that to get rich you will need to be paid based on results.

Poor people trade their time for money. The problem with this strategy is that your time is limited. This means that you invariably end up breaking Wealth Rule #1, which states, "Never have a ceiling on your income." If you choose to get paid for your time, you are pretty much killing your chances for wealth.

WEALTH PRINCIPLE:
Never have a ceiling on your income.

This rule also applies to personal service businesses, where, again, you generally get paid for your time. That's why lawyers, accountants, and consultants who are not yet partners in their firm—and therefore don't share in the business profits—make a moderate living at best.

Suppose you are in the pen business and you get an order for fifty thousand pens. If this were the case, what would you do? You'd simply call your supplier, order fifty thousand pens, send them off, and happily count your profits. On the other hand, suppose you are a massage therapist and you're fortunate enough to have fifty thousand people lined up outside your door all wanting a massage from you. What do you do? You kill yourself for not being in the pen business. What else can you do? Try explaining to the last person in line that you may be running "a little late," as in their appointment is Tuesday at 3:15, four decades from now!

I'm not suggesting there's anything wrong with being in a personal service business. Just don't expect to get rich anytime soon unless you create a way to duplicate or leverage yourself.

At my seminars, I often meet salaried or hourly wage employees who complain to me that they're not getting paid what they're worth. My response is "In whose opinion? I'm sure your boss thinks you're being compensated fairly. Why don't you get off the salary treadmill and ask to be paid based fully or partially on your performance? Or, if that is not possible, why not work for yourself? Then you'll know you're making exactly what you're worth." Somehow, this advice doesn't seem to appease these people, who are obviously terrified of testing their "true" value in the marketplace.

The fear most people have of being paid based on their results is often just a fear of breaking out of their old conditioning. In my experience, most people who are stuck in the steady-paycheck rut have past programming that tells them this is the "normal" way to get paid for your work.

You can't blame your parents. (I guess you can if you're a good victim.) Most parents tend to be overly protective, so it's only natural for them to want their kids to have a secure existence. As you've probably already found out, any work that doesn't provide a steady paycheck usually produces the infamous parental response "When are you going to get a real job?"

I remember, when my parents asked me that question, thank goodness my reply was "Hopefully never!" My mother was devastated. My father, however, said, "Good for you. You'll never get rich working on straight salary for someone else. If you're going to get a job, make sure you get paid on percentage. Otherwise, go work for yourself!"

I too encourage you to work "for yourself." Start your own business, work on commission, get a percentage of revenue or company profits, or get stock options. Whatever your vehicle, make certain you create a situation that allows you to get paid based on your results.

Personally, I believe just about everyone should own their own business, be it full-time or part-time. The first reason is that by far, *the vast majority of millionaires became rich by being in their own business.*

Secondly, it's extremely difficult to create wealth when the tax man is grabbing almost half of everything you earn. When you own a business, you can save a small fortune in taxes by writing off a portion of your expenses for such things as your car, travel, education, and even your home. For that reason alone, it's worth having your own business.

If you don't have a brilliant business idea, not to worry: you can use someone else's. First, you can become a commissioned salesperson. Selling is one of the world's highest-paid professions. If you're good, you can earn a fortune. Second, you can join a network marketing company. There are dozens of excellent ones, and they have in place all of the products and systems you need to get started immediately. For just a few bucks, you can become a distributor and have all the benefits of owning a business with few of the administrative hassles.

If it resonates with you, network marketing can be a dynamite vehicle for wealth. But, and this is a big but, don't think for a minute that you're going to get a free ride. Network marketing will only work if you do. It will take training, time, and energy to succeed. But if you do, incomes in the range of $20,000 to $50,000 per month—that's right, per month—are not uncommon. In any case, just signing up and becoming a part-time distributor will give you some excellent tax advantages, and who knows, maybe you'll enjoy the product enough to offer it to others and end up making a nice income to boot.

Another option is exchanging your "job" for a "contract" position. If your employer is willing, he or she can hire your company instead of you to do basically what you're doing now. A few legal requirements have to be fulfilled, but for the most part, if you add one or two more clients, even part-time, you can get paid as a business owner instead of an employee and enjoy business-owner tax benefits. Who knows, those part-time clients may grow to become full-time clients, which would then give you the opportunity to leverage yourself, hire other people to get all the work done, and eventually you'll be running your own full-on business.

You might think, "My employer would never go for that." I wouldn't be too sure about that. You have to understand, it costs a company a fortune to have an employee. Not only do they have to pay salary or wages, but they have to pay a whack of money on top of that to the government, often to the tune of 25 percent or more above what the employee earns. Add to that the cost of the benefits package that most employees get, and you've probably got a 50 percent savings to a company that chooses to hire you as an independent consultant. Of course you won't be eligible for many of the benefits you got as an employee, but for what you save in taxes alone, you can buy the best of what you need on your own.

In the end, the only way to earn what you're really worth is to get paid based on your results. Once again, my dad said it best: "You'll never get rich working on straight salary for someone else. If you're going to get a job, make sure you get paid on percentage. Otherwise, go work for yourself!"

Now that's sage advice!

DECLARATION: Place your hand on your heart and say . . .

"I choose to get paid based on my results."

Touch your head and say . . .

"I have a millionaire mind!"

MILLIONAIRE MIND ACTIONS

1. If you are currently in a job getting paid based on an hourly wage or salary, create and propose a compensation plan to your employer that would allow you to get paid at least partly based on your individual results as well as the results of the company.

   If you own your own business, create a compensation plan that allows your employees or even primary suppliers to get paid based more on their results and the results of your company.

   Put these plans into action immediately.

2. If you are currently in a job and not being paid what you are worth based on the results you are producing, consider starting start your own business. You can begin part-time. You could easily join a network marketing company or become a coach, teaching others what you know, or offer your independent consulting services back to the company you originally worked for, but this time, paid on performance and results rather than only for your time.

Success Story from Sean Nita

Dear Harv,

I can't explain how grateful we are that we were introduced to you by one of my wife's friends. At the time I'd just received a $10,000 cut in pay. We were desperately looking for options, as we were not making ends meet anymore.

At the Millionaire Mind Intensive, we learned the tools that helped us create financial freedom. Once we put the tools in place, miracles started to happen. We were able to purchase five homes within the next year. All with a minimum profit of at least $18,000 each. The fifth house had a profit of $300,000, six times my previous yearly salary! I was able to quit my job of fourteen years and become a full-time real estate investor, giving me the free time to be with my family and friends.

Your method of teaching at the cellular level has been a great key to our success. I cannot wait for what is ahead. I only wish I'd learned this when I was in my twenties.

Thank you.

Sincerely,
Sean Nita
Seattle, WA

Wealth File #12

Rich people think "both."
Poor people think "either/or."

Rich people live in a world of abundance. Poor people live in a world of limitations. Of course, both live in the same physical world, but the difference is in their perspective. Poor and most middle-class people come from scarcity. They live by mottos such as "There's only so much to go around, there's never enough, and you can't have everything." And although you may not be able to have "everything," as in all the things in the world, I do think you can certainly have "everything you really want."

Do you want a successful career or a close relationship with your family? Both! Do you want to focus on business or have fun and play? Both! Do you want money or meaning in your life? Both! Do you want to earn a fortune or do the work you love? Both! Poor people always choose one, rich people choose both.

Rich people understand that with a little creativity you can almost always figure out a way to have the best of both worlds. From now on, when confronted with an either/or alternative, the quintessential question to ask yourself is "How can I have both?" This question will change your life. It will take you from a model of scarcity and limitation to a universe of possibilities and abundance.

This doesn't just pertain to things you want, it pertains to all areas of life. For example, right now, I'm preparing to deal with an unhappy supplier that believes my company, Peak Potentials, should pay for certain expenses they've had that weren't originally agreed to. My feeling is that estimating his costs is his business not mine, and if he's incurred higher expenses, that's something he has to deal with. I'm more than willing to negotiate a new agreement for next time, but I'm big on keeping agreements that were already made. Now in my "broke" days, I'd go into this discussion with the goal of making my point and making sure I don't pay this guy one cent more than we agreed upon. And even though I'd like to keep him as a supplier, this would probably end up in a huge argument. I'd go in thinking either he wins or I win.

Today, however, because I've trained myself to think in terms of "both," I'm going into this discussion completely open to creating a situation where I'm not going to pay him any more money *and* he's going to be extremely happy with the arrangements we do make. In other words, my goal is to have *both*!

Here's another example. Several months ago I decided to purchase a vacation home in Arizona. I scoured the area I was interested in, and every real estate agent told me, if I wanted three bedrooms plus a den in that vicinity, I'd have to pay over a million dollars. My intention was to keep my investment in this home under a million. Most people would either lower their expectations or raise their budget. I held out for both. I recently got a call that the owners of a house in the exact location I wanted, with the number of rooms I wanted, had reduced their price $200,000 to under a million. Here is another tribute to the intention of having both!

Finally, I always told my parents that I didn't want to slave away at work I didn't enjoy and that I would "get rich doing what I love." Their response was the usual: "You're living in a dream world. Life is not a bowl of cherries." They said,

"Business is business, pleasure is pleasure. First you take care of making a living, then, if there's any time left over, you can enjoy your life."

I remember thinking to myself, "Hmm, if I listen to them, I'll end up like them. No. I'm gonna have *both*!" Was it tough? You bet. Sometimes I'd have to work at a job I hated for a week or two so I could eat and pay the rent. But I never lost my intention of having "both." I never got stuck long-term in a job or business I didn't like. Eventually I did become rich doing what I loved. Now that I know it can be done, I continue to pursue only the work and projects that I love. Best of all, I now have the privilege of teaching others to do the same.

Nowhere is "both" thinking more important than when it comes to money. Poor and many middle-class people believe that they have to choose between money and the other aspects of life. Consequently they've rationalized a position that money is not as important as other things.

Let's set the record straight. Money is important! To say that it's not as important as any of the other things in life is ludicrous. What's more important, your arm or your leg? Could it be that *both* are important?

Money is a lubricant. It enables you to "slide" through life instead of having to "scrape" by. Money brings freedom—freedom to buy what you want, and freedom to do what you want with your time. Money allows you to enjoy the finer things in life as well as giving you the opportunity to help others have the necessities in life. Most of all, having money allows you not to have to spend your energy worrying about not having money.

Happiness is important too. Again, here's where poor and middle-class people get confused. Many believe money and happiness are mutually exclusive, that either you can be rich *or* you can be happy. Again, this is nothing more than "poor" programming.

People who are rich in every sense of the word understand that you have to have *both*. Just as you have to have both your arms and your legs, you have to have money *and* happiness.

You Can Have Your Cake and Eat It Too!

So here's another major difference between rich people, middle-class people, and poor people:

Rich people believe "You can have your cake and eat it too."

Middle-class people believe "Cake is too rich, so I'll only have a little piece."

Poor people don't believe they deserve cake, so they order a doughnut, focus on the hole, and wonder why they have "nothing."

WEALTH PRINCIPLE:
Rich people believe
"You can have your cake and eat it too."
Middle-class people believe
"Cake is too rich, so I'll only have a little piece."
Poor people don't believe they deserve cake,
so they order a doughnut, focus on the hole,
and wonder why they have "nothing."

I ask you, what is the use of having your "cake" if you can't eat it? What exactly are you supposed to do with it? Put it on your mantel and look at it? Cake is meant to be eaten and enjoyed.

Either/or thinking also trips up people who believe that "if I have more, then someone else will have less." Again, this is nothing more than fear-based, self-defeating programming. The notion that the wealthy people of the world have and are somehow hoarding all the money, so there's none left for anyone else, is preposterous. First, this belief assumes that there is a limited supply of money. I'm not an economist, but from what I can see, they just keep printing more of the stuff every day. The actual money supply hasn't been tied to any real asset for decades. So even if the wealthy had all the money today, tomorrow there'd be millions, if not billions, more available.

The other thing people with this limited belief don't seem to realize is that the same money can be used over and over, to create value for everyone. Let me give you an example I've used in our seminars. I'll ask five people to come onstage and bring an item with them. I ask them to stand in a circle. Then I give a $5 bill to the first person and ask them to buy something from person number 2 for that money. Suppose they buy a pen. So now person number 1 has a pen and person number 2 has the $5. Person 2 now uses the same $5 bill to buy, say, a clipboard from person number 3. Then number 3 uses the same $5 bill to buy a notebook from number 4. I hope you get the picture and the point. The exact same $5 was used to bring value to each person that had it. That same $5 went through five different people and created $5 worth of value for each and a total of $25 in value for the group. That $5 did not get depleted and as it circled around, created value for everyone.

The lessons are clear. First, money does not get depleted; you can use the same money again and again for years and years and thousands and thousands of people. Second, the more money you have, the more you can put into the circle, which means other people then have more money to trade for more value.

This is exactly the opposite of either/or-based thinking. To the contrary, when you have money and use it, you and the person you spend it with *both* have the value. Put bluntly, if you're so worried about other people and making sure they get their share (as if there is a share), do what it takes to get rich so you can spread more money around.

If I can be an example for anything, it would be that you can be a kind, loving, caring, generous, and spiritual person *and* be really frickin' rich. I strongly urge you to dispel the myth that money is in any way bad or that you will be less "good" or less "pure" if you are wealthy. That belief is absolute "salami" (in case you're tired of baloney), and if you keep eating it, you won't just be fat, you'll be fat *and* broke. Hey, what do you know, another example of *both*!

My friends, being kind, generous, and loving has nothing to do with what is or isn't in your wallet. Those attributes come from what is in your heart. Being pure and spiritual have nothing to do with what is or isn't in your bank account; those attributes come from what's in your soul. To think money makes you good or bad, one way or another, is either/or thinking and just plain "programmed garbage" that is not supportive to your happiness and success.

It's also not supportive to those around you, especially to children. If you're that adamant about being a good person, then be "good" enough not to infect the next generation with the disempowering beliefs you may inadvertently have adopted.

If you really want to live a life without limits, whatever the situation, let go of either/or thinking and maintain the intention to have "both."

DECLARATION: Place your hand on your heart and say . . .

"I always think 'both.' "

Touch your head and say . . .

"I have a millionaire mind!"

MILLIONAIRE MIND ACTIONS

1. Practice thinking and creating ways of having "both." Whenever alternatives are presented to you, ask yourself, "How can I have both?"

2. Become aware that money in circulation adds to everyone's life. Each time you spend money, say to yourself, "This money will go through hundreds of people and create value for all of them."

3. Think of yourself as a role model for others—showing that you can be kind, generous, loving, *and* rich!

Wealth File #13

Rich people focus on their net worth. Poor people focus on their working income.

When it comes to money, people in our society typically ask, "How much do you make?" Seldom do you hear the question "What is your net worth?" Few people talk this way, except of course at the country club.

In country clubs, the financial discussion almost always centers around net worth: "Jim just sold his stock options; he's worth over three million. Paul's company just went public; he's worth eight million. Sue just sold her business; she's now worth twelve million." At the country club, you're not going to hear, "Hey, did you hear that Joe got a raise? Yeah, and a two percent cost-of-living allowance to boot?" If you did hear that, you'd know you're listening to a *guest* for the day.

WEALTH PRINCIPLE:
The true measure of wealth is net worth,
not working income.

The true measure of wealth is net worth, not working income. Always has been, always will be. Net worth is the financial value of everything you own. To determine your net worth, add up the value of everything you own, including your cash and investments such as stocks, bonds, real estate, the current value of your business if you own one, the value of your residence if you own it, and then subtract everything you owe. Net worth is the ultimate measure of wealth because, if necessary, what you own can eventually be liquidated into cash.

Rich people understand the huge distinction between working income and net worth. Working income is important, but it is only one of the four factors that determine your net worth. The four net worth factors are:

1. Income

2. Savings

3. Investments

4. Simplification

Rich people understand that building a high net worth is an equation that contains all four elements. Because all of these factors are essential, let's examine each one.

Income comes in two forms: working income and passive income. Working income is the money earned from active work. This includes a paycheck from a day-to-day job, or for an entrepreneur, the profits or income taken from a business. Working income requires that you are investing your own time and labor to earn money. Working income is important because, without it, it is almost impossible to address the other three net worth factors.

Working income is how we fill up our financial "funnel," so to speak. All things being equal, the more working income you earn, the more you can save and invest. Although working income is critical, again it is only valuable as a part of the entire net worth equation.

Unfortunately, poor and many middle-class people focus exclusively on working income, out of the four factors. Consequently, they end up with a low or no net worth.

Passive income is money earned without you actively working. We will discuss passive income in greater detail a little later, but for now, consider it another stream of income filling up the funnel, which can then be used for spending, saving, and investing.

Savings is also imperative. You can earn wads of money.

But if you don't keep any of it, you will never create wealth. Many people have a financial blueprint that is wired for spending. Whatever money they have, they spend. They choose immediate gratification over long-term balance. Spenders have three mottoes. Their first motto is "It's only money." Therefore, money is something they don't have much of. Their second motto is "What goes around, comes around." At least they hope so, because their third motto is "Sorry, I can't right now. I'm broke." Without creating income to fill the funnel and savings to keep it there, it is impossible to address the next net worth factor.

Once you've begun saving a decent portion of your income, then you can move to the next stage and make your money grow through investing. Generally, the better you are at investing, the faster your money will grow and generate a greater net worth. Rich people take the time and energy to learn about investing and investments. They pride themselves on being excellent investors or at least hiring excellent investors to invest for them. Poor people think investing is only for rich people, so they never learn about it and stay broke. Again, every part of the equation is important.

Our fourth net worth factor may well be the "dark horse" of the bunch, because few people recognize its importance in creating wealth. This is the factor of "simplification." It goes hand in hand with saving money, whereby you consciously create a lifestyle in which you need less money to live on. By decreasing your cost of living, you increase your savings and the amount of funds available for investing.

To illustrate the power of simplification, here's the story of one of our Millionaire Mind participants. When Sue was only twenty-three, she made a wise choice: she purchased a home. She paid just under $300,000 at the time. Seven years later, in a sizzling hot market, Sue sold her home for over $600,000, meaning she profited over $300,000. She considered buying a new home, but after attending the Millionaire Mind Intensive Seminar, she recognized that if she invested her money in a secure second mortgage at 10 percent interest and simplified her lifestyle, she could actually be quite comfortable living on the earnings from her investments and not have to work ever again. Instead of purchasing a new home, she moved in with her sister. Now, at thirty years of age, Sue is financially free. She won her independence not through earning a ton of money, but by consciously scaling back her personal overhead. Yes, she still works—because she enjoys it—but she doesn't have to. In fact, she only works six months of the year. The rest of the time she spends in Fiji, first because she loves it, and second, she says, her money goes even further there. Because she lives with the locals rather than the tourists, she doesn't spend a lot. How many people do you know who would love to spend six months of each year living on a tropical island, never having to work again, at the ripe old age of thirty? How about forty? Fifty? Sixty? Ever? It's all because Sue created a simple lifestyle and, consequently, doesn't need a fortune to live on.

So, what will it take for you to be happy financially? If you need to live in a mansion, have three vacation homes, own ten cars, take annual trips around the world, eat caviar, and drink the finest champagne to enjoy your life, that's fine, but recognize you've set your bar pretty darn high, and it may take you a long, long time to get to a point where you're happy.

On the other hand, if you don't need all the "toys" to be happy, you'll probably reach your financial goal a lot sooner.

Again, building your net worth is a four-part equation. As

an analogy, imagine driving a bus with four wheels. What would the ride be like if you were driving on one wheel only? Probably slow, bumpy, full of struggle, sparks, and going in circles. Does that sound familiar? Rich people play the money game on all four wheels. That's why their ride is fast, smooth, direct, and relatively easy.

By the way, I use the analogy of a bus because once you are successful, your goal might be to bring others along on the ride with you.

Poor and most middle-class people play the money game on one wheel only. They believe that the only way to get rich is to earn a lot of money. They believe that only because they've never been there. They don't understand Parkinson's Law, which states, "Expenses will always rise in direct proportion to income."

Here's what's normal in our society. You have a car, you make more money, and you get a better car. You have a house, you make more money, and you get a bigger house. You have clothes, you make more money, and you get nicer clothes. You have holidays, you make more money, and you spend more on holidays. Of course there are a few exceptions to this rule . . . very few! In general, as income goes up, expenses almost invariably go up too. That's why income alone will never create wealth.

This book is called *Secrets of the Millionaire Mind*. Does *millionaire* refer to income or net worth? Net worth. Therefore, if your intention is to be a millionaire or more, you must focus on building your net worth, which, as we've discussed, is based on much more than just your income.

Make it a policy to know your net worth to the penny. Here's an exercise that can change your financial life forever.

Take a blank sheet of paper and title it "Net Worth."

Then create a simple chart that begins with zero and ends with whatever your net worth objective is. Note your current net worth as it is today. Then every ninety days, enter your new net worth. That's it. If you do this, you will find yourself getting richer and richer. Why? Because you will be "tracking" your net worth.

Remember: what you focus on expands. As I often say in our training, "Where attention goes, energy flows and results show."

WEALTH PRINCIPLE:
"Where attention goes, energy flows
and results show."

By tracking your worth, you are focusing on it, and because what you focus on expands, your net worth will expand. By the way, this law goes for every other part of your life: what you track increases.

To that end, I encourage you to find and work with a good financial planner. These professionals can help you track and build your net worth. They will assist you in organizing your finances and introduce you to a variety of vehicles for saving and growing your money.

The best way to find a good planner is to seek a referral from a friend or associate who is happy with the person he or she uses. I'm not saying to take everything your planner says as gospel. But I am suggesting that you find a qualified professional with the skills to help you plan and track your finances. A good planner can provide you with the tools, software, knowledge, and recommendations to help you build the kind of investing habits that will produce wealth.

Generally, I recommend finding a planner who works with an array of financial products rather than just insurance or just mutual funds. In that way, you can find out about a variety of options, then decide what's right for you.

> **DECLARATION:** Place your hand on your heart and say . . .
>
> *"I focus on building my net worth!"*
>
> Touch your head and say . . .
>
> *"I have a millionaire mind!"*

MILLIONAIRE MIND ACTIONS

1. Focus on all four net worth factors: increasing your income, increasing your savings, increasing your investment returns, and decreasing your cost of living by simplifying your lifestyle.

2. Create a net worth statement. To do this, add the current dollar value of everything you own (your assets) and subtract the total value of everything you owe (your liabilities). Commit to tracking and revising this statement each quarter. Again, by virtue of the law of focus, what you track will increase.

3. Hire a financial planner who is highly successful and works with a well-known, reputable company. Again, the best way to find a great financial planner is to ask friends and associates for their referrals.

Special Bonus: Go to **www.millionairemindbook.com** and click on "FREE BOOK BONUSES" to receive your free "net worth tracking sheet."

Wealth File #14

Rich people manage their money well.
Poor people mismanage their money well.

Thomas Stanley, in his best-selling book, *The Millionaire Next Door,* surveyed millionaires from across North America and reported on who they are and how they attained their wealth. The results can be summarized in one short sentence: "Rich people are good at managing their money." Rich people manage their money well. Poor people mismanage their money.

Wealthy people are not any smarter than poor people; they just have different and more supportive money habits. As we discussed in Part I of this book, these habits are primarily based on our past conditioning. So first, if you're not managing your money properly, you were probably programmed not to manage money. Second, there's a better than good chance you don't know how to manage your money in a way that's easy and effective. I don't know about you, but where I went to school, Money Management 101 wasn't offered. Instead we learned about the War of 1812, which of course is something I use every single day.

It may not be the most glamorous of topics, but it comes down to this: the single biggest difference between financial success and financial failure is how well you manage your money. It's simple: to master money, you must manage money.

Poor people either mismanage their money or they avoid the subject of money altogether. Many people don't like to manage their money because, first, they say it restricts their freedom, and second, they say they don't have enough money to manage.

As for the first excuse, managing money does not restrict your freedom—to the contrary, it promotes it. Managing your money allows you to eventually create financial freedom so that you never have to work again. To me, that's real freedom.

As for those who use the "I don't have enough money to manage" rationale, they're looking through the wrong end of the telescope. Rather than say "when I have plenty of money, I'll begin to manage it," the reality is "when I begin to manage it, I'll have plenty of money."

Saying "I'll start managing my money as soon as I get caught up" is like an overweight person saying "I'll start exercising and dieting as soon as I lose twenty pounds." It's putting the cart before the horse, which leads to going nowhere . . . or even backward! First you start properly handling the money you have, then you'll have more money to handle.

In the Millionaire Mind Intensive Seminar, I tell a story that hits most people right between the eyes. Imagine you're walking along the street with a five-year-old. You come across an ice cream store and go inside. You get the child a single scoop of ice cream on a cone because they don't have any cups. As the two of you walk outside, you notice the cone wobbling in the child's tiny hands and, all of a sudden, plop. The ice cream falls out of the cone onto the pavement.

The child begins to cry. So back you go into the store, and just as you're about to order for the second time, the child notices a colorful sign with a picture of the "triple scooper" cone. The child points to the picture and excitedly screams, "I want that one!"

Now here's the question. Being the kind, loving, and generous person that you are, would you go ahead and get this child the triple scooper? Your initial response might be "sure." However, when considering the question a little more deeply, most of our seminar participants respond, "No." Because why would you want to set the child up to fail? The child couldn't even handle a single scoop, how could the child possibly handle a triple scoop?

The same holds true when it comes to the universe and you. We live in a kind and loving universe, and the rule is "Until you show you can handle what you've got, you won't get any more!"

WEALTH PRINCIPLE:
Until you show you can handle what you've got,
you won't get any more!

You must acquire the habits and skills of managing a small amount of money before you can have a large amount. Remember, we are creatures of habit, and therefore the habit of managing your money is more important than the amount.

WEALTH PRINCIPLE:
The habit of managing your money
is more important than the amount.

So how exactly do you manage your money? At the Millionaire Mind Intensive Seminar, we teach what many believe to be an amazingly simple and effective money management method. It's beyond the scope of this book to go over every detail; however, let me give you a couple of the basics so you can get started.

Open a separate bank account designated your Financial Freedom Account. Put 10 percent of every dollar you receive (after taxes) into this fund. This money is only to be used for investments and buying or creating passive-income streams. The job of this account is to build a golden goose that lays golden eggs called passive income. And when do you get to spend this money? *Never!* It is never spent—only invested. Eventually, when you retire, you get to spend the income from the fund (the eggs), but never the principal itself. In this way, it always keeps growing and you can never go broke.

One of our students, named Emma, recently told me her story. Two years ago Emma was about to claim bankruptcy. She didn't want to; however, she felt she had no other option. She was in debt beyond what she could handle. Then she attended the Millionaire Mind Intensive Seminar and learned about the money management system. Emma said, "This is it. This is how I'm going to get out of this mess!"

Emma, like all the participants, was told to divide her money into several different accounts. "That's just great," she thought to herself. "I don't have any money to divide up!" But since she wanted to try, Emma decided to divide up $1 a month into the accounts. Yes, that's right, only $1 a month.

Based on the allocation system we teach, using that one dollar, she put ten cents into her FFA (Financial Freedom Account). The first thing she thought to herself was "How the heck am I supposed to become financially free on ten cents a month?" So she committed to doubling that dollar every month. The second month she divided up $2, the third month $4, then $8, $16, $32, $64, and so on until the twelfth month was $2,048 that she was dividing up each month.

Then, two years later, she began to collect some amazing fruits from her efforts. She was able to put $10,000 directly into her Financial Freedom Account! She had developed the habit of managing her money so well that, when a bonus check of $10,000 came her way, she didn't need the money for anything else!

Emma is now out of debt and on her way to becoming financially free. All because she took action with what she'd learned, even if it was only with $1 a month.

It doesn't matter if you have a fortune right now or virtually nothing. What does matter is that you immediately begin to manage what you've got, and you'll be in shock at how soon you get more.

I had another student at the Millionaire Mind Intensive Seminar say, "How can I manage my money when I'm borrowing money to live on as it is?" The answer is, borrow an extra dollar and manage that dollar. Even if you are borrowing or finding just a few dollars a month, you must manage that money, because more than a "physical" world principle is at play here: this is also a spiritual principle. Money miracles will occur once you demonstrate to the universe that you can handle your finances properly.

In addition to opening a Financial Freedom bank account, create a Financial Freedom jar in your home and deposit money into it every day. It could be $10, $5, $1, a single penny, or all your loose change. The amount doesn't matter; the habit does. The secret again is to place daily "attention" on your objective of becoming financially free. Like attracts like, money attracts more money. Let this simple jar become your "money magnet," attracting more and more money and opportunities for financial freedom into your life.

Now, I'm sure this isn't the first time you've heard the advice to save 10 percent of your money for long-term investing, but it may be the first time you've heard that you must have an equal and opposite account specifically designed for you to "blow" money and play.

One of the biggest secrets to managing money is balance. On one side, you want to save as much money as possible so you can invest it and make more money. On the other side, you need to put another 10 percent of your income into a "play" account. Why? Because we are holistic in nature. You cannot affect one part of your life without affecting the others. Some people save, save, save, and while their logical and responsible self is fulfilled, their "inner spirit" is not. Eventually this "fun-seeking" spirit side will say, "I've had enough. I want some attention too," and sabotage their results.

On the other hand, if you spend, spend, spend, not only will you never become rich, but the responsible part of you will eventually create the situation where you don't even enjoy the things you spend your money on, and you'll end up feeling guilty. The guilt will then cause you to unconsciously overspend as a way of expressing your emotions. Although you might feel better temporarily, soon it's back to guilt and shame. It's a vicious cycle, and the only way to prevent it is to learn how to manage your money in a way that works.

Your play account is primarily used to nurture yourself— to do the things you wouldn't normally do. It's for the extraspecial things like going to a restaurant and ordering a bottle of their finest wine or champagne. Or renting a boat for the day. Or staying in a high-class hotel for an extravagant night of fun and frolic.

The play account rule is that it must be spent every month. That's right! Each month you have to blow all the money in that account in a way that makes you feel rich. For example, imagine walking into a massage center, dumping all the money from your account on the counter, pointing to the massage therapists, and saying, "I want *both* of you on me. With the hot rocks and the frickin' cucumbers. After that, bring me lunch!"

Like I said, extravagant. The only way most of us will ever continue to follow our saving plan is by offsetting it with a playing plan that will reward us for our efforts. Your play account is also designed to strengthen your "receiving" muscle. It also makes managing money a heck of a lot more fun. In addition to the play account and the financial freedom account, I advise that you create four more accounts. The other accounts include:

10 percent into your Long-Term Savings for Spending Account

10 percent into your Education Account

50 percent into your Necessities Account

10 percent into your Give Account

Again, poor people think it's all about income; they believe you have to earn a fortune to get rich. Again, that's male-cow manure! The fact is that if you manage your money following this program, you can become financially free on a relatively small income. If you mismanage your money, you can't become financially free, even on a huge income. That is why so many high-income professionals—doctors, lawyers, athletes, and even accountants—are basically broke, because it's not just about what comes in, it's about what you do with what comes in.

One of our attendees, John, told me that when he first heard about the money management system, he thought, "How boring! Why would anyone spend their precious time doing that?" Then later during the seminar he finally realized if he wanted to be financially free someday, especially sooner than later, he too would have to manage his money, just like the rich.

John had to learn this new habit because it definitely wasn't natural for him. He said it reminded him of when he was training for triathlons. He was really good at swimming and cycling; however, he hated the running. It hurt his feet, knees, and back. He was stiff after every training session. He was always out of breath and his lungs burned every time, even if he wasn't going fast! He used to dread running. However, he knew that if he was to become a top triathlete, he had to learn to run and accept it as part of what it took to succeed. Whereas in the past John avoided running, he now decided to run every day. After a few months, he began enjoying running and actually looked forward to it each day.

This is exactly what happened to John in the arena of money management. He started out hating every minute of it but grew to actually like it. Now he looks forward to getting his paycheck and dividing it into the different accounts! He also enjoys watching how his net worth has gone from zero to over $300,000 and is growing daily.

It comes down to this: either you control money, or it will control you. To control money, you must manage it.

WEALTH PRINCIPLE:
Either you control money, or it will control you.

I love hearing seminar graduates share how much more confident they feel around money, success, and themselves once they begin managing their money properly. The best part is that this confidence transfers into other parts of their lives and enhances their happiness, their relationships, and even their health.

Money is a big part of your life, and when you learn how to get your finances under control, all areas of your life will soar.

DECLARATION: Place your hand on your heart and say . . .

"I am an excellent money manager."

Touch your head and say . . .

"I have a millionaire mind!"

MILLIONAIRE MIND ACTIONS

1. Open your Financial Freedom bank account. Put 10 percent of all your income (after taxes) into this account. This money is never to be spent, only invested to produce passive income for your retirement.

2. Create a Financial Freedom jar in your home and deposit money into it every day. It could be $10, $5, $1, a single penny, or all your loose change. Again, this will put daily attention on your financial freedom, and where attention goes, results show.

Success Story from Christine Kloser

From: Christine Kloser
To: T. Harv Eker

To put it simply, after attending T. Harv Eker's Millionaire Mind Intensive, my relationship with money completely changed, and my business grew by 400 percent within one year.

Most importantly, my husband and I finally "got" how important it was to save the first 10 percent of our income every month, no matter what. Now, I'm happy to say, we've saved more in the few years after attending Harv's program than we had in the previous fifteen years!

Plus, the techniques we learned for solving money issues in our relationship has kept us "money argument" free ever since.

Harv's money management system is easy to follow and *works*!

To your success.

3. Open a play account or have a play jar in your home where you deposit 10 percent of all your income. Along with your play account and your financial freedom account, open four more accounts and deposit the following percentages into each:

10 percent into your Long-Term Savings for Spending Account

10 percent into your Education Account

50 percent into your Necessities Account

10 percent into your Give Account

4. Whatever money you have, begin managing it now. Do not wait another day. Even if you only have a dollar. Manage that dollar. Take ten cents and put it into your FFA jar, and another ten cents and put it into your play jar. This action alone will send a message to the universe that you are ready for more money. Of course if you can manage more, manage more.

Wealth File #15

Rich people have their money work hard for them. Poor people work hard for their money.

If you're like most people, you grew up being programmed that you "have to work hard for money." Chances are good, however, that you didn't grow up with the conditioning that it was just as important to make your money "work hard for you."

No question, working hard is important, but working hard alone will never make you rich. How do we know that? Take a look in the real world. There are millions—no, make that billions—of people who slave away, working their tails off all day and even all night long. Are they all rich? No! Are most of them rich? No! Are a lot of them rich? No! Most of them are broke or close to it. On the other hand, whom do you see lounging around the country clubs of the world? Who spends their afternoons playing golf, tennis, or sailing? Who spends their days shopping and their weeks vacationing? I'll give you three guesses and the first two don't count.

Rich people, that's who! So let's get this straight: the idea that you have to work hard to get rich is bogus!

The old Protestant work ethic states "a dollar's work for a dollar's pay." There's nothing wrong with that adage except that they forgot to tell us what to do with that "dollar's pay." Knowing what to do with that dollar is where you move from hard work to *smart* work.

Rich people can spend their days playing and relaxing because they work smart. They understand and use leverage. They employ other people to work for them and their money to work for them.

Yes, in my experience, you do have to work hard for your money. For rich people, however, this is a temporary situation. For poor people, it's permanent. Rich people understand that "you" have to work hard until your "money" works hard enough to take your place. They understand that *the more your money works, the less you will have to work.*

Remember, money is energy. Most people put work energy in and get money energy out. People who achieve financial freedom have learned how to substitute their investment of work energy with other forms of energy. These forms include other people's work, business systems at work, or investment capital at work. Again, first you work hard for money, then you let money work hard for you.

When it comes to the money game, most people don't have a clue as to what it takes to win. What's your goal? When do you win the game? Are you shooting for three square meals a day, $100,000 a year in income, becoming a millionaire, becoming a multimillionaire? At the Millionaire Mind Intensive Seminar, the goal of the money game we teach is to "never have to work again . . . unless you choose to," and that if you work, you work "by choice, not by necessity."

In other words, the goal is to become "financially free" as quickly as possible. My definition of financial freedom is simple: it is *the ability to live the lifestyle you desire without having to work or rely on anyone else for money.*

Notice there is a good chance that your desired lifestyle is going to cost money. Therefore, to be "free," you will need to earn money without working. We refer to income without work as passive income. To win the money game, the goal is to earn enough *passive* income to pay for your desired lifestyle. In short, you become financially free when your passive income exceeds your expenses.

I have identified two primary sources of passive income. The first is "money working for you." This includes investment earnings from financial instruments such as stocks, bonds, T-bills, money markets, mutual funds, as well as owning mortgages or other assets that appreciate in value and can be liquidated for cash.

The second major source of passive income is "business working for you." This entails generating ongoing income from businesses where you do not need to be personally involved for that business to operate and yield an income. Examples include rental real estate; royalties from books, music, or software; licensing your ideas; becoming a franchisor; owning storage units; owning vending or other types of coin-operated machines; and network marketing, to name just a few. It also includes setting up any business under the sun or moon that is systematized to work without you. Again, it's a matter of energy. The idea is that the business is working and producing value for people, instead of you.

Network marketing, for example, is an amazing concept. First, it doesn't usually require you to put up a lot of up-front capital. Second, once you've done the initial work, it allows you to enjoy ongoing residual income (another form of income without you working), year after year after year. Try creating that from a regular nine-to-five job!

I can't overemphasize the importance of creating passive income structures. It's simple. Without passive income you can never be free. But, and it's a big but, did you know that most people have a tough time creating passive income? There are three reasons. First, conditioning. Most of us were actually programmed *not* to earn passive income. When you were somewhere between thirteen and sixteen years old and you needed money, what did your parents tell you? Did they say, "Well, go out there and earn some passive income?" Doubtful! Most of us heard, "Go to work," "Go get a job," or something to that effect. We were taught to "work" for money, making passive income abnormal for most of us.

Second, most of us were never taught how to earn passive income.

In my school, Passive Income 101 was another subject that was never offered. This time I got to take woodworking and metalworking (notice both still entailed "working") and make the perfect candleholder for my mom. Since we didn't learn about creating passive income structures in school, we learned it elsewhere, right? Doubtful. The end result is that most of us don't *know* much about it, and therefore don't *do* much about it.

Finally, since we were never exposed to or taught about passive income and investing, we have never given it much attention. We have largely based our career and business choices on generating working income. If you understood from an early age that a primary financial goal was to create passive income, wouldn't you reconsider some of those career choices?

I'm always recommending to folks choosing or changing their business or career to find a direction where generating streams of passive income is natural and relatively easy. This is especially important today because so many people work in service businesses where they have to be there personally to make money. There's nothing wrong with being in a personal service business, other than that unless you get on your investment horse pretty soon and do exceptionally well, you'll be trapped into working forever.

By choosing business opportunities that immediately or eventually produce passive income, you'll have the best of both worlds—working income now and passive income later. Refer back a few paragraphs to review some of the passive business income options we discussed.

Unfortunately, almost everyone has a money blueprint that is set *for* earning working income and *against* earning passive income. This attitude will be radically changed after you attend the Millionaire Mind Intensive Seminar, where using experiential techniques, we change your money blueprint so that earning a massive passive income is normal and natural for you.

Rich people think long-term. They balance their spending on enjoyment today with investing for freedom tomorrow. Poor people think short-term. They run their lives based on immediate gratification. Poor people use the excuse "How can I think about tomorrow when I can barely survive today?" The problem is that, eventually, tomorrow will become today; if you haven't taken care of today's problem, you'll be saying the same thing again tomorrow too.

To increase your wealth, you either have to earn more or live on less. I don't see anyone putting a gun to your head telling you the house you have to live in, the kind of car you have to drive, the clothes you have to wear, or the food you have to eat. You have the power to make choices. It's a matter of priorities. Poor people choose *now,* rich people choose *balance.* I think about my in-laws.

For twenty-five years my wife's parents owned a variety store, a low-end version of a 7-Eleven and a lot smaller. Most of their income came from the sale of cigarettes, candy bars, ice cream bars, gum, and sodas. They didn't even sell lottery tickets in those days. The average sale was less than a dollar. In short, they were in a "penny" business. Still, they saved most of those pennies. The didn't eat out; they didn't buy fancy clothes; they didn't drive the latest car. They lived comfortably but modestly and eventually paid off their mortgage and even bought half of the plaza the store was located within. At the age of fifty-nine, by saving and investing "pennies," my father-in-law was able to retire.

I hate to be the one to have to tell you this, but for the most part, buying things for immediate gratification is nothing more than a futile attempt to make up for our dissatisfaction in life. More often than not, "spending" money you don't have comes from "expending" emotions you *do* have. This syndrome is commonly known as retail therapy. Overspending and the need for immediate gratification have little to do with the actual item you're buying, and everything to do with lack of fulfillment in your life. Of course, if overspending isn't coming from your immediate emotions, it arises from your money blueprint.

According to Natalie, another of our students, her parents were the ultimate cheapskates! They used coupons for everything. Her mother had a file box full of coupons all sorted by category. Her father had a fifteen-year-old car that was rusting, and Natalie was embarrassed to be seen in it, especially when her mom picked her up from school. Anytime she got in the car, Natalie prayed that no one was looking. On vacation, her family never stayed in a motel or hotel; they didn't even fly, but drove eleven days across the country and camped the whole way, every year!

Everything was "too expensive." The way they acted, Natalie thought her parents were broke. But her dad earned what she believed was a lot of money at the time, $75,000 a year. She was confused.

Because she hated their stingy habits, she became the opposite. She wanted everything to be high-class and expensive. When she moved out on her own and started making her own money, she didn't even realize it, but in a flash, she had spent all the money she had, and then some!

Natalie had credit cards, membership cards, you name it. She racked up all of them to the point where she couldn't even pay the minimums anymore! That's when she took the Millionaire Mind Intensive Seminar and she says it saved her life.

At the Millionaire Mind Intensive, during the section where we identify your "money personality," Natalie's whole world changed. She recognized why she had been spending all her money. It was a form of resentment toward her parents for being so cheap. It was also to prove to herself and the world that she wasn't cheap. Since the course, with her blueprint changed, Natalie says she no longer has the urge to spend her money in "stupid" ways.

Natalie related she was recently walking through a mall and noticed this gorgeous light brown suede and fur coat hanging in the window display of one of her favorite stores. Immediately her mind said, "That coat would look great on you, especially with your blond hair. You need that; you don't have a really nice, dressy winter coat." So she walked into the store, and as she was trying it on, she noticed the price tag, $400. She had never spent that much on a coat before. Her mind said, "So what, the coat looks gorgeous on you! Get it. You'll make the money up later."

This is where she says she discovered how profound the Millionaire Mind Intensive is. Almost as soon as her mind suggested that she buy the coat, her new and more supportive mind "file" came up and said, "You'd be much better off putting that four hundred dollars toward your FFA account! What do you need this coat for? You already have a winter coat that's okay for now."

Before she knew it, she was putting the coat on hold until the next day instead of buying it right there in the moment as usual. She never went back to get the coat.

Natalie realized that her mental "material gratification" files had been replaced with "financial freedom" files. She wasn't programmed to spend anymore. She now knows it's fine to take the best of what her parents modeled for her and save money, and at the same time, to treat herself to nice things with her play account.

Natalie then sent her parents to the course so they could be more balanced as well. She's thrilled to report, they now stay in motels (not hotels yet), they bought a new car, and in learning how to make their money work for them, they've retired as millionaires.

Natalie now understands that she doesn't have to be as "cheap" as her parents were to become a millionaire. But she also knows that if she spends her money unconsciously as before, she'll never be financially free. Natalie said, "It feels amazing to have my money and my mind under control."

Again, the idea is to have your money work as hard for you as you do for it, and that means you have to save and invest rather than make it your mission in life to spend it all. It's almost funny: rich people have a lot of money and spend a little, while poor people have a little money and spend a lot.

Long-term versus short-term: poor people work to earn money to live today; rich people work to earn money to pay for their investments, which will pay for their future.

Rich people buy assets, things that will likely go up in value. Poor people buy expenses, things that will definitely go down in value. Rich people collect land. Poor people collect bills.

I'll tell you the same thing I tell my kids: "Buy real estate." It's best if you can purchase property that can produce positive cash flow, but as far as I'm concerned, any real estate is better than no real estate. Sure, real estate has its ups and downs, but in the end, be it five, ten, twenty, or thirty years from now, you can bet it will be worth a heck of a lot more than it is today, and it could be all you need to get rich.

Buy what you can afford now. If you need more capital to get involved, you can partner with people you trust and know well. The only way to get in trouble with real estate is to overextend yourself or have to sell in a down market. If you heed my earlier advice and manage your money properly, the likelihood of this happening will be extremely slim and likely none. As the saying goes, "Don't wait to buy real estate, buy real estate and wait."

Since I gave you a previous example involving my in-laws, it's only fair I give you an example involving my own parents. My parents weren't poor, but they barely made the middle class. My dad worked extremely hard and my mom wasn't physically well, and so she stayed home with us kids. My dad was a carpenter and recognized that all the builders who employed him were developing land they had purchased years and years ago. He also recognized they were all fairly rich. My parents too saved their pennies and eventually had enough to buy a three-acre parcel of land about twenty miles outside the city in which they lived. It cost them $60,000. Ten years later, a developer decided he wanted to build a strip mall on that property. My parents sold for $600,000. Less their original investment, that's an average earnings of $54,000 a year from their investment, while my dad earned only about $15,000 to a high of $20,000 a year from his job. Of course they are retired now and live quite comfortably, but I guarantee that without the purchase and sale of this property, they would have been living by the skin of their teeth. Thank goodness my father recognized the power of investment and especially the value of investing in real estate. Now you know why I collect land.

While poor people see a dollar as a dollar to trade for something they want right now, rich people see every dollar as a "seed" that can be planted to earn a hundred more dollars, which can then be replanted to earn a thousand more dollars. Think about it. Every dollar you spend today may actually cost you a hundred dollars tomorrow. Personally, I consider each of my dollars to be investment "soldiers," and their mission is "freedom." Needless to say, I'm careful with my "freedom fighters" and don't get rid of them quickly or easily.

WEALTH PRINCIPLE:
Rich people see every dollar as a "seed"
that can be planted to earn a hundred
more dollars, which can then be replanted
to earn a thousand more dollars.

The trick is to get educated. Learn about the investment world. Become familiar with a variety of different investment vehicles and financial instruments, such as real estate, mortgages, stocks, funds, bonds, currency exchange, the whole gamut. Then choose one primary area in which to become an expert. Begin investing in that area and then diversify into more, later.

It comes down to this: poor people work hard and spend all their money, which results in their having to work hard forever. Rich people work hard, save, and then invest their money so they never have to work hard again.

DECLARATION: Place your hand on your heart and say . . .

"My money works hard for me and makes me more and more money."

Touch your head and say . . .

"I have a millionaire mind!"

MILLIONAIRE MIND ACTIONS

1. Get educated. Take investment seminars. Read at least one investment book a month. Read magazines such as *Money, Forbes, Barron's,* and the *Wall Street Journal.* I'm not suggesting you follow their advice, I'm sug-

gesting you get familiar with what financial options are out there. Then choose an arena to become an expert in and begin investing in that area.

2. Change your focus from "active" income to "passive" income. List at least three specific strategies with which you could create income without working, in either the investment or the business field. Begin researching and then take action on these strategies.

3. Don't wait to buy real estate. Buy real estate and wait.

Wealth File #16

Rich people act in spite of fear.
Poor people let fear stop them.

Earlier in this book we discussed the Process of Manifestation. Let's review the formula: thoughts lead to feelings, feelings lead to actions, actions lead to results.

Millions of people "think" about getting rich, and thousands and thousands of people do affirmations, visualizations, and meditations for getting rich. I meditate almost every day. Yet I've never sat there meditating or visualizing and had a bag of money drop on my head. I guess I'm just one of those unfortunate ones who actually has to *do* something to be a success.

Affirmations, meditations, and visualizations are all wonderful tools, but as far as I can tell, none of them on its own is going to bring you real money in the real world. In the real world, you have to take real "action" to succeed. Why is action so critical?

Let's go back to our Process of Manifestation. Look at

thoughts and feelings. Are they part of the inner world or outer world? Inner world. Now look at results. Are they part of the inner or outer world? Outer world. That means action is the "bridge" between the inner world and the outer world.

WEALTH PRINCIPLE:
Action is the "bridge" between the inner world
and the outer world.

So if action is so important, what prevents us from taking the actions we know we need to take?

Fear!

Fear, doubt, and worry are among the greatest obstacles, not only to success, but to happiness as well. Therefore, one of the biggest differences between rich people and poor people is that rich people are willing to act in spite of fear. Poor people let fear stop them.

Susan Jeffers even wrote a fantastic book about this, entitled *Feel the Fear and Do It Anyway.* The biggest mistake most people make is waiting for the feeling of fear to subside or disappear before they are willing to act. These people usually wait forever.

One of our most popular programs is the Enlightened Warrior Training Camp. In that training, we teach that a true warrior can "tame the cobra of fear." It doesn't say kill the cobra. It doesn't say get rid of the cobra, and it certainly doesn't say run away from the cobra. It says "tame" the cobra.

WEALTH PRINCIPLE:
A true warrior can "tame the cobra of fear."

It's imperative to realize that it is not necessary to try to get rid of fear in order to succeed. Rich and successful people have fear, rich and successful people have doubts, rich and successful people have worries. They just don't let these feelings stop them. Unsuccessful people have fears, doubts, and worries, then let those feelings stop them.

WEALTH PRINCIPLE:
It is not necessary to try to get rid of fear
in order to succeed.

Because we are creatures of habit, we need to practice acting in spite of fear, in spite of doubt, in spite of worry, in spite of uncertainty, in spite of inconvenience, in spite of discomfort, and even to practice acting when we're not in the mood to act.

I remember teaching an evening seminar in Seattle, and near the end, I was letting people know about the upcoming three-day Millionaire Mind Intensive Seminar being held in Vancouver. This one fella stands up and says, "Harv, I've had at least a dozen of my family and friends attend the course, and the results have been absolutely phenomenal. Every one of them is ten times happier than before, and they're all on the road to financial success. They all said it was life changing, and if you were holding the course in Seattle, I'd definitely come too."

I thanked him for his testimonial and then asked if he was open to some coaching. He agreed and I said, "I have only three words for you." He cheerfully replied, "What are they?" To which I tersely responded, *"You're frickin' broke!"*

Then I asked him how he was doing financially. He

sheepishly replied, "Not too good." Of course I replied, "No kidding." I then began ranting and raving at the front of the room: "If you are going to let a three-hour drive or a three-hour flight or a three-day trek stop you from doing something you need and want to do, then what else will stop you? Here's the easy answer: *anything!* Anything will stop you. Not because of the size of the challenge but because of the size of you!

"It's simple," I continued. "Either you are a person who will be stopped, or you are a person who won't be stopped. You choose. If you want to create wealth or any other kind of success, you have to be a warrior. You have to be willing to do whatever it takes. *You have to 'train' yourself to not be stopped by anything.*

"Getting rich is not always convenient. Getting rich is not always easy. In fact, getting rich can be pretty damn hard. But so what? One of the key enlightened warrior principles states, 'If you are willing to do only what's easy, life will be hard. But if you are willing to do what's hard, life will be easy.' Rich people don't base their actions on what's easy and convenient; that way of living is reserved for the poor and most of the middle class."

WEALTH PRINCIPLE:
If you are willing to do only what's easy,
life will be hard. But if you are willing to do
what's hard, life will be easy.

The tirade was over. The crowd was silent.

Later, the fella who'd started the entire discussion came up and thanked me profusely for "opening his eyes." Of course he registered for the course (even though it was in Vancouver), but what was really funny was overhearing him on the phone as I was leaving, fervently giving the exact same speech I had just given him to one of his friends on the other end of the line. I guess it worked because the next day he called in with three more registrations. They were all from the East Coast . . . and they were all coming to Vancouver!

Now that we've addressed convenience, what about discomfort? Why is acting in spite of discomfort so important? Because "comfortable" is where you're at now. If you want to move to a new level in your life, you must break through your comfort zone and practice doing things that are not comfortable.

Let's suppose you are currently leading a level 5 life and you want to move to a level 10 life. Level 5 and below are within your comfort zone, but level 6 and above are outside your box, in your "uncomfort" zone. Meaning, to get to a level 10 life from a level 5 life, you will have to travel through your uncomfort zone.

Poor people and most of the middle class are not willing to be uncomfortable. Remember, being comfortable is their biggest priority in life. But let me tell you a secret that only rich and highly successful people know: being comfortable is highly overrated. Being comfortable may make you feel warm, fuzzy, and secure, but it doesn't allow you to grow. To grow as a person you have to expand your comfort zone. The only time you can actually grow is when you are *outside* your comfort zone.

Let me ask you a question. The first time you tried something new, was it comfortable or uncomfortable? Usually uncomfortable. But what happened afterward? The more you did it, the more comfortable it became, right? That's how it goes. Everything is uncomfortable at the beginning, but if you stick with it and continue, you will eventually move through the uncomfort zone and succeed. Then you will have a new, expanded comfort zone, which means you will have become a "bigger" person.

Again, the only time you are actually growing is when you are uncomfortable. From now on, whenever you feel uncomfortable, instead of retreating back into your old comfort zone, pat yourself on the back and say, "I must be growing," and continue moving forward.

WEALTH PRINCIPLE:
The only time you are actually growing
is when you are uncomfortable.

If you want to be rich and successful, you'd better get comfortable with being uncomfortable. Consciously practice going into your uncomfort zone and doing what scares you. Here's an equation I want you to remember for the rest of your life: CZ = WZ.

It means your "comfort zone" equals your "wealth zone."

By expanding your comfort zone, you will expand the size of your income and wealth zone. The more comfortable you have to be, the fewer risks you will be willing to take, the fewer opportunities you will take advantage of, the fewer people you will meet, and the fewer new strategies you will try. Do you catch my drift? The more comfort becomes your priority, the more contracted you become with fear.

On the contrary, when you are willing to s-t-r-e-t-c-h yourself, you expand your opportunity zone, and this allows you to attract and hold more income and wealth. Again, when you have a large "container" (comfort zone), the universe will rush to fill the space. Rich and successful people have a big comfort zone, and they are constantly expanding it to be able to attain and hold more wealth.

Nobody ever died of discomfort, yet living in the name of comfort has killed more ideas, more opportunities, more actions, and more growth than everything else combined. Comfort kills! If your goal in life is to be comfortable, I guarantee two things. First, you will never be rich. Second, you will never be happy. Happiness doesn't come from living a lukewarm life, always wondering what could have been. Happiness comes as a result of being in our natural state of growth and living up to our fullest potential.

Try this. The next time you are feeling uncomfortable, uncertain, or afraid, instead of shrinking and retreating back to safety, press forward. Notice and experience the feelings of discomfort, recognizing that they are only feelings—and that they do not have the power to stop you. If you doggedly continue in spite of discomfort, you will eventually reach your goal.

Whether the feelings of discomfort ever subside doesn't matter. In fact, when they do lessen, take it as a sign to increase your objective, because the minute you get comfortable, you have stopped growing. Again, to grow yourself to your fullest potential, you must always be living at the edge of your box.

And because we are creatures of habit, we must *practice*. I urge you to practice acting in spite of fear, practice acting in spite of inconvenience, practice acting in spite of discomfort, and practice acting even when you're not in the mood.

By doing so, you will quickly move to a higher level of life. Along the way, make sure you check your bank account, because, guaranteed, that will be growing quickly too.

At this point in some of my evening seminars I ask the audience, "How many of you are willing to practice acting in spite of fear and discomfort?" Usually everyone puts his or her hand up (probably because they're scared to death I'm going to "pick" on them). Then I say, "Talk is cheap! Let's see whether you mean it." I then pull out a wooden arrow with a steel-pointed tip and explain that as a practice for this discipline, you're going to break this arrow with your throat. I then demonstrate how the steel point goes into the soft part of your throat, while another person holds the other end of the arrow against their outstretched palm. The idea is to walk straight into the arrow and break it using only your throat before it pierces through your neck.

At this point most people are in shock! Sometimes I pick one volunteer to do this exercise, sometimes I hand out arrows to everyone. I've done audiences where over a thousand people are breaking arrows!

Can this feat be accomplished? Yes. Is it scary? You bet. Is it uncomfortable? Absolutely. But again, the idea is that fear and discomfort do not stop you. The idea is to practice, to train yourself to do whatever it takes, and to act in spite of anything that might be in your way.

Do most people break the arrow? Yes, everyone who walks into it with 100 percent commitment breaks it. However, those who walk into it slowly, halfheartedly, or not at all, don't.

After the arrow exercise I ask people, "How many of you found the arrow easier to break physically than what your mind made it up to be?" All agree it was actually a lot easier than they thought it would be. Why is this so? Here comes one of the most important lessons you will ever learn.

Your mind is the greatest soap-opera scriptwriter in history. It makes up incredible stories, usually based in dramas and disasters, of things that never happened and probably never will. Mark Twain said it best: "I've had thousands of problems in my life, most of which never actually happened."

One of the most important things you can ever understand is that *you are not your mind.* You are much bigger and greater than your mind alone. Your mind is a part of you just as your hand is a part of you.

Here's a thought-provoking question: What if you had a hand that was just like your mind? It was scattered all over the place, it was always beating you up, and it never shut up. What would you do with it? Most people answer something like "Cut it off!" But your hand is a powerful tool, so why would you cut it off? The real answer of course is you'd want to control it, manage it, and train it to work for you instead of against you.

Training and managing your own mind is the most important skill you could ever own, in terms of both happiness and success, and that's exactly what we've been doing with this book and will continue to do with you should you attend one of our live programs.

WEALTH PRINCIPLE:
Training and managing your own mind is the
most important skill you could ever own,
in terms of both happiness and success.

How do you train your mind? You start with observation. Notice how your mind consistently produces thoughts that are not supportive to your wealth and happiness. As you identify those thoughts, you can begin to consciously replace those nonempowering thoughts with empowering ones. Where do you find these empowering ways of thinking? Right here, in this book. Every one of the declarations in this book is an empowering and successful way of thinking.

Adopt these ways of thinking, being, and attitudes as your own. You don't have to wait for a formal invitation. Decide right now that your life would be better if you chose to think in the ways we've been describing in this book, instead of through the self-defeating mental habits of the past. Make a decision that from now on, your thoughts do not run you, you run your thoughts. From now on, your mind is not the captain of the ship, you are the captain of the ship, and your mind works for you.

You can choose your thoughts.

You have the natural ability to cancel any thought that is not supporting you, at any time. You can also install self-empowering thoughts at any time, simply by choosing to focus on them. You have the power to control your mind.

As I mentioned earlier, at one of my seminars one of my closest friends and best-selling author Robert Allen said something quite profound: "No thought lives in your head rent-free."

What that means is that you will pay for negative thoughts. You will pay in money, in energy, in time, in health, and in your level of happiness. If you want to quickly move to a new level of life, begin dividing your thoughts into one of two categories—empowering or disempowering. Observe the thoughts you have, and determine if they are supportive to your happiness and success or not supportive. Then choose to entertain only empowering thoughts while refusing to focus on disempowering ones. When a nonsupportive thought bubbles up, say "Cancel" or "Thank you for sharing" and replace it with a more supportive way of thinking. I call this process power thinking, and mark my words, if you practice it, your life will never be the same again. That is a promise!

So what is the difference between "power thinking" and "positive" thinking? The distinction is slight but profound. To me, people use positive thinking to pretend that everything is rosy, when they really believe that it's not. With power thinking, we understand that everything is neutral, that nothing has meaning except for the meaning we give it, and that we are going to make up a story and give something its meaning.

This is the difference between positive thinking and power thinking. With positive thinking, people believe that their thoughts are true. Power thinking recognizes that our thoughts are not true, but since we're making up a story anyway, we might as well make up a story that supports us. We don't do this because our new thoughts are "true" in an absolute sense, but because they are more useful to us and feel a heck of a lot better than nonsupportive ones.

Before we leave this section, I must warn you—do not attempt the arrow-break exercise at home. The exercise has to be set up in a specific way or you could hurt yourself as well as others around you. At our programs we use protective equipment. If you have an interest in these types of breakthrough exercises, see the description of the Enlightened

Warrior Training Camp on our Web site. This program will give you all you can handle and more!

DECLARATIONS: Place your hand on your heart and say . . .

"I act in spite of fear."
"I act in spite of doubt."
"I act in spite of worry."
"I act in spite of inconvenience."
"I act in spite of discomfort."
"I act when I'm not in the mood."

Touch your head and say . . .

"I have a millionaire mind!"

MILLIONAIRE MIND ACTIONS

1. List your three greatest worries, concerns, or fears regarding money and wealth. Challenge them. For each, write down what you would do if the situation you fear actually happened. Could you still survive? Could you make a comeback? Chances are that the answers are yes. Now quit worrying and start getting rich!

2. Practice getting out of your comfort zone. Intentionally make decisions that are uncomfortable for you. Speak to people you normally wouldn't speak to, ask for a raise in your job or raise your prices in your business, wake up an hour earlier each day, walk in the woods at night. Take the Enlightened Warrior Training. It will train you to be unstoppable!

3. Employ "power thinking." Observe yourself and your thought patterns. Entertain only thoughts that sup-

port your happiness and success. Challenge the little voice in your head whenever it tells you "I can't" or "I don't want to" or "I don't feel like it." Don't allow this fear-based, comfort-based voice to get the better of you. Make a pact with yourself that whenever the voice tries to stop you from doing something that would be supportive to your success, you will do it anyway, to show your mind that you are the boss, not it. Not only will you increase your confidence dramatically, but eventually this voice will get quieter and quieter as it recognizes it has little effect on you.

Success Story from Andrew Wilton

Harv,

My name is Andrew Wilton and I am eighteen years old. I have just completed my first year of university. I attended the Millionaire Mind Intensive two years ago and I have been using the techniques I learned there ever since.

This past February for reading week, while my friends were working or visiting their families, using the money that I had saved through your methods, I was able to spend ten days on the southern coast of Spain. What an experience!

I wouldn't have had the financial freedom to go wherever I wanted and do whatever I wanted if I hadn't implemented the strategies I learned at the MMI.

Thank you, Harv.

Wealth File #17

Rich people constantly learn and grow. Poor people think they already know.

At the beginning of my live seminars, I introduce people to what I call "the three most dangerous words in the English language." Those words are "I know that." So how do you know if you know something? Simple. If you *live* it, you know it. Otherwise, you heard about it, you read about it, or you talk about it, but you don't know it. Put bluntly, if you're not really rich and really happy, there's a good chance you still have some things to learn about money, success, and life.

As I explained at the beginning of this book, during my "broke" days, I was fortunate to get some advice from a multimillionaire friend who had some compassion for my plight. Remember what he said to me: "Harv, if you're not as successful as you'd like to be, there's something you don't know." Fortunately, I took his suggestion to heart and went from being a "know-it-all" to a "learn-it-all." From that moment on, everything changed.

Poor people are often trying to prove that they're right. They put on a mask as if they've got it all figured out, and it's just some stroke of bad luck or a temporary glitch in the universe that has them broke or struggling.

One of my more famous lines is "You can be right *or* you can be rich, but you can't be both." Being "right" means having to hold on to your old ways of thinking and being. Unfortunately, these are the ways that got you exactly where you are now. This philosophy also pertains to happiness, in that "you can be right *or* you can be happy."

WEALTH PRINCIPLE:
You can be right *or* you can be rich,
but you can't be both.

There's a saying that author and speaker Jim Rohn uses that makes perfect sense here: "If you keep doing what you've always done, you'll keep getting what you've always got." You already know "your" way, what you need is to know some new ways. That's why I wrote this book. My goal is to give you some new mental files to add to the ones you already have. New files mean new ways of thinking, new actions, and therefore new results.

That's why it's imperative you continue to learn and grow.

Physicists agree that nothing in this world is static. Everything alive is constantly changing. Take any plant. If a plant isn't growing, it is dying. It's the same with people as well as all other living organisms: if you are not growing, you are dying.

One of my favorite sayings is by author and philosopher Eric Hoffer, who said, "The learners shall inherit the earth while the learned will be beautifully equipped to live in a world that no longer exists." Another way of saying that is, if you're not continuously learning, you will be left behind.

Poor people claim they can't afford to get educated due to lack of time or money. On the other hand, rich people relate to Benjamin Franklin's quote: "If you think education is expensive, try ignorance." I'm sure you've heard this before, "knowledge is power," and power is the ability to act.

Whenever I offer the Millionaire Mind Intensive program, I find it interesting that it's usually the people who are the most broke who say, "I don't need the course," "I don't have the time," or "I don't have the money." Meanwhile, the millionaires and multimillionaires all register and say, "If I can learn just one new thing or make one improvement, it's worth it." By the way, if you don't have the time to do the things you want to do or need to do, you're most probably a modern slave. And if you don't have the money to learn how to be successful, you probably need it more than anyone. I'm sorry, but saying "I don't have the money" just doesn't cut it. When will you have the money? What is going to be different a year or two years or five years from now? Here's the easy answer: nothing! And you'll be saying the exact same words again at that time.

The only way I know for you to have the money you want is to learn how to play the money game inside and out. You need to learn the skills and strategies to accelerate your income, to manage money, and to invest it effectively. The definition of insanity is doing the same thing over and over and expecting different results. Look, if what you've been doing were working, you'd already be rich and happy. Anything else your mind conjures up as a response is nothing more than an excuse or justification.

I hate to be so in your face about it, but the way I see it, that's my job. I believe a good coach will always ask more of you than you will ask of yourself. Otherwise, why the heck do you need one? As a coach, my goal is to train you, inspire you, encourage you, coax you, and have you observe, in full living color, what is holding you back. In short, to do whatever it takes to move you to the next level in your life. If I have to, I'll rip you apart and then piece you back together in a way that works. I'll do whatever it takes to make you ten times happier and a hundred times as rich. If you're looking for Pollyanna, I'm not your guy. If you want to move quickly and permanently, let's continue.

Success is a learnable skill. You can learn to succeed at anything. If you want to be a great golfer, you can learn how to do it. If you want to be a great piano player, you can learn how to do it. If you want to be truly happy, you can learn how to do it. If you want to be rich, you can learn how to do it. It doesn't matter where you are right now. It doesn't matter where you are starting from. What matters is that you are willing to learn.

One of my better-known quotes is "Every master was once a disaster." Here's an example. A while ago, I had an Olympic skier in my seminar. When I made that statement, he stood up and asked to share. He was adamant, and for some reason I thought he was going to vehemently disagree. To the contrary, he told everyone the story of how when he was a kid, he was the worst skier of all his buddies. How they sometimes wouldn't call him to go skiing with them because he was so slow. To fit in, he went to the mountain early each weekend and took lessons. Pretty soon he not only kept up with his buddies, he surpassed them. He then got involved in the racing club and learned from a top-ranked coach. His exact words were "I might be a master skier now, but I definitely started out as a disaster. Harv's absolutely right. You can learn to succeed at anything. I learned how to succeed at skiing, and my next goal is to learn how to succeed with money!"

WEALTH PRINCIPLE:
"Every master was once a disaster."
—T. Harv Eker

No one comes out of the womb a financial genius. Every rich person learned how to succeed at the money game, and so can you. Remember, your motto is, if they can do it, I can do it!

Becoming rich isn't as much about getting rich financially as about whom you have to become, in character and mind, to get rich. I want to share a secret with you that few people know: the fastest way to get rich and stay rich is to work on developing *you*! The idea is to grow yourself into a "successful" person. Again, your outer world is merely a reflection of your inner world. You are the root; your results are the fruits.

There's a saying I like: "You take yourself with you wherever you go." If you grow yourself to become a successful person, in strength of character and mind, you will naturally be successful in anything and everything you do. You will gain the power of absolute choice. You will gain the inner power and ability to choose any job, business, or investment arena and know you'll be a success. This is the essence of this book. When you are a level 5 person, you get level 5 results. But if you can grow into a level 10 person, you will get level 10 results.

Heed this warning, however. If you don't do the inner work on yourself, and somehow you make a lot of money, it would most likely be a stroke of luck and there's a good chance you'd lose it. But if you become a successful "person" inside and out, you'll not only make it, you'll keep it, grow it, and most important, you'll be truly happy.

Rich people understand the order to success is BE, DO, HAVE.

Poor and middle-class people believe the order to success is HAVE, DO, BE.

Poor and most middle-class people believe "If I *have* a lot of money, then I could *do* what I want and I'd *be* a success."

Rich people understand, "If I *become* a successful person, I will be able to *do* what I need to do to *have* what I want, including a lot of money."

Here's something else only rich people know: the goal of creating wealth is not primarily to have a lot of money, the goal of creating wealth is to help you grow yourself into the best person you can possibly be. In fact, that is the goal of all goals, to grow yourself as a person. World-renowned singer and actress Madonna was asked why she kept changing her persona, her music, and her style every year. She responded that music was her way to express her "self" and that reinventing herself each year forces her to grow into the kind of person she wants to be.

In short, success is not a "what," it's a "who." The good news is that "who" you are is totally trainable and learnable. I should know. By no means am I perfect or even close to it, but when I look at who I am today as opposed to who I was twenty years ago, I can see a direct correlation between "me and my wealth" (or lack of it) then and "me and my wealth" now. I learned my way to success and so can you. That's why I'm in the training business. I know from personal experience that virtually any person can be trained to succeed. I was trained to succeed, and now I've been able to train tens of thousands of others to succeed. Training works!

I've found that another key difference between rich people and poor and middle-class people is that rich people are *experts* in their field. Middle-class people are mediocre in their field, and poor people are poor in their field. How good are you at what you do? How good are you at your job? How good are you at your business? Do you want a totally unbiased way of knowing? Look at your paycheck. That will tell you everything. It's simple: *to get paid the best, you must be the best.*

WEALTH PRINCIPLE:
To get paid the best, you must be the best.

We recognize this principle in the professional sports world every day. Generally, the best players in every sport earn the most. They also make the most money on endorsements. This same principle also holds true in both the business and financial worlds. Whether you choose to be a business owner, a professional, a network marketing distributor, whether you're in commissioned sales or a salaried job, whether you're an investor in real estate, stocks, or anything else, all things being equal: the better you are at it, the more you'll earn. This is just another reason why being a continuous learner and enhancing your skill in whatever arena you are in is imperative.

On the topic of learning, it's worth noting that rich people not only continue to learn, they make sure they learn from those who have already been where they themselves want to go. One of the things that made the biggest difference for me personally was whom I learned from. I always made it a point to learn from true masters in their respective fields—not those who claimed to be experts, but those who had real-world results to back up their talk.

Rich people take advice from people who are richer than they are. Poor people take advice from their friends, who are just as broke as they are.

I recently had a meeting with an investment banker who

wanted to do business with me. He was suggesting I place several hundred thousand dollars with him to get started. He then asked me to forward him my financial statements so he could make his recommendations.

I looked him in the eye and said, "Excuse me, but don't you have this backward? If you want me to hire you to handle my money, wouldn't it be more appropriate for you to forward me *your* financial statements? And if you're not really rich, don't bother!" The man was in shock. I could tell that no one had ever questioned his own net worth as a stipulation for investing with him.

It's absurd. If you were going to climb Mount Everest, would you hire a guide who's never been to the summit before, or would it be smarter to find someone who's made it to the top several times and knows exactly how to do it?

So, yes, I am absolutely suggesting you put serious attention and energy into continuously learning and, at the same time, be cautious of whom you are learning and taking advice from. If you learn from those who are broke, even if they're consultants, coaches, or planners, there's only one thing they can teach you—how to be broke!

By the way, I highly recommend you consider hiring a personal success coach. A good coach will keep you on track in doing what you've said you want to do. Some coaches are "life" coaches, meaning they handle the gamut of everything, while other coaches have specialties that might include personal or professional performance, finances, business, relationships, health, and even spirituality. Again, find out your prospective coach's background to ensure the coach has demonstrated success in the arenas of importance to you.

Just as there are successful paths to climbing Mount Everest, there are proven routes and strategies for creating high income, fast financial freedom, and wealth. You have to be willing to learn them and use them.

Again, as part of our Millionaire Mind Money Management method, I strongly suggest that you put 10 percent of your income into an Education Fund. Use this money specifically for courses, books, tapes, CDs, or any other way you choose to educate yourself, whether through the formal education system, private training companies, or personalized, one-on-one coaching. Whatever method you choose, this fund ensures you will always have the wherewithal to learn and grow instead of repeating the poor person's refrain of "I already know." The more you learn, the more you earn . . . and you can take that to the bank!

> **DECLARATION:** Place your hand on your heart and say . . .
>
> *"I am committed to constantly learning and growing."*
>
> Touch your head and say . . .
>
> *"I have a millionaire mind!"*

MILLIONAIRE MIND ACTIONS

1. Commit to your growth. Each month read at least one book, listen to one educational tape or CD, or take a seminar on money, business, or personal development. Your knowledge, your confidence, and your success will soar!

2. Consider hiring a personal coach to keep you on track.

3. Attend the Millionaire Mind Intensive. This amazing event has transformed the lives of thousands and thousands of people and will transform your life too!

"So What the Heck
Do I Do Now?"

SO WHAT NOW? WHAT DO YOU DO? WHERE DO YOU
start?

I've said it before, and I'll say it again and again and again: "Talk is cheap." I hope you enjoyed reading this book, but more important, I hope you use its principles to dramatically enhance your life. In my experience, however, reading alone will not make the difference you are looking for. Reading is a start, but if you want to succeed in the real world, it's going to be your actions that count.

In Part I of this book, I introduced the concept of your money blueprint. It's simple: your financial blueprint will determine your financial destiny. Make certain you do each of the exercises I suggested in the arenas of verbal programming, modeling, and specific incidents, in order to begin changing your blueprint to one that supports financial success. I also encourage you to do the declarations I suggested each and every day.

In Part II of this book, you learned seventeen specific ways that rich people think differently from poor and middle-class people. I recommend you commit each of these "wealth files" to memory by repeating their declarations daily. This will root these principles into your mind. Eventually you will find yourself looking at life and especially money very differently. From there you will make new choices and decisions and create new results. To speed up this process, make sure you do the action exercises given at the end of each of the wealth files.

These action exercises are imperative. For change to be permanent, it must occur on a cellular basis—your brain's wiring must be remade. This means you have to put the material into practice. Not just read about it, not just talk about it, and not just think it, but actually do it.

Beware of the little voice in your head saying something like "Exercises, schmexercises, I don't need or have time for exercises." Notice who is doing the talking here? The conditioned mind, that's who! Remember, its job is to keep you right where you are, in your comfort zone. Don't listen to it. Do the action exercises, do your declarations, and watch your life skyrocket!

I also suggest you reread this book from beginning to end at least once a month for the next year. "What?" your little voice might be screaming. "I've already read the book, why do I need to read it over and over again?" Good question, and the answer is simple: repetition is the mother of learning. Again, the more you study this book, the faster the concepts will become natural and automatic for you.

Be sure to visit **www.millionairemindbook.com** and click on "FREE BOOK BONUSES" to receive several valuable gifts that include:

- A printable list of declarations suitable for framing
- The Millionaire Mind "thought of the week"

- The Millionaire Mind "action reminder"
- The Millionaire Mind "net worth tracking sheet"
- A printout of your "Commitment to Wealth"

As I stated earlier, I learned my way to success, so now it's my turn to assist others. My mission is to "educate and inspire people to live in their 'higher self' based in courage, purpose, and joy versus fear, need, and obligation."

I am truly blessed to have seminars, workshops, and camps that transform people's lives quickly and permanently. I'm thrilled to have been able to help over 250,000 people become richer and happier. From my heart to yours, I invite you to attend the three-day Millionaire Mind Intensive Seminar. This event will take you to an entirely new level of success. The course is where we actually change your money blueprint right on the spot.

In one incredible weekend you will break through whatever is holding you back from reaching your full financial potential. You will walk out of the program with a brand-new outlook on life, on money, on your relationships, and on yourself. Many attendees count the Millionaire Mind Intensive as one of the most important experiences of their life. It's fun, it's exciting, and it's packed with profound knowledge and essential financial skills. You will meet hundreds of like-minded people from all over the world, many of whom could become business associates and lifelong friends. This course is so crucial for you to attend that, for a limited time, the publishers of this book and I have decided to provide a scholarship to you and a family member to attend the course free as our guests. That's right, both of you come *free*!

See the following pages for more details about this offer to you.

Well, that's it for now. Thank you for spending your precious time reading this book. I wish you tremendous success and true happiness, and I look forward to meeting you in person soon.

For your freedom,

T. Harv Eker

T. Harv Eker's Three-Day Millionaire Mind Intensive Seminar Free!

As a thank-you for purchasing *Secrets of the Millionaire Mind,* T. Harv Eker is offering a scholarship for you and a family member to attend the three-day Millionaire Mind Intensive Seminar as his complimentary guests. That is a total value of $2,590—for free!

These guest seats are available to purchasers of T. Harv Eker's *Secrets of the Millionaire Mind* published by Harper-Business. This is a limited time offer and the course must be completed by the date shown on the website www.million-airemindbook.com. There will be an administration fee or deposit taken upon registration, and this offer is made on a space-available. All seating is first come, first serve. To assure your spot, please register immediately at **www.millionaire-mindbook.com**.

At the Millionaire Mind Intensive weekend program, you

will expand upon the insights provided in this book by learning:

- How to permanently change your money blueprint for natural and automatic success.

- A step-by-step process for winning the money game, so that you never have to work again . . . unless you choose to.

- Rarely revealed high-income and wealth-creation strategies.

- How to quadruple your speed to financial freedom.

- The world's easiest and most effective money-management method.

- The habits of truly wealthy people.

- The underlying cause of almost all financial problems.

- Twelve ways to earn passive income so you can make money while you sleep.

- How to release your hidden emotional blocks to wealth.

- How to recognize your "money personality" so you can build on your strengths and overcome your weaknesses.

By the end of the course, you will have the inner capacity to create wealth and, more important, to keep your wealth and grow it. Best of all, the same inner strategies that work to create success with money work to enhance your inner peace and happiness as well.

Whether you are currently a millionaire, middle-class, or broke, if you're not 100 percent satisfied with your income, your net worth, or your level of happiness, and you know you have more potential than your results are showing, then register for the Millionaire Mind Intensive Seminar today. This course will change your life. Register now at **www.million airemindbook.com**.

"The Millionaire Mind Seminar is life-changing. I urge every one of my students to attend this powerful course. It is incredible."

—Robert G. Allen, *New York Times* number one best-selling author, *Nothing Down Real Estate* and *Multiple Streams of Income,* coauthor, *The One Minute Millionaire*

"Harv Eker is one of the most extraordinary trainers in the world today! Harv's experiential techniques are transformational, and he creates amazing results every time he speaks!"

—Mark Victor Hansen, cocreator, *Chicken Soup for the Soul®,* more than 70 million sold; coauthor, *The One Minute Millionaire*

"T. Harv Eker is an electrifying speaker! He has the ability to transfix an audience, motivate and enlighten them, and give them information in a way that they absorb it fully. I've seen and heard a lot of speakers; none are as dynamic as T. Harv Eker!"

—Jay Conrad Levinson, author of the *Guerrilla Marketing* book series, more than 14 million sold

MILLIONAIRE MIND
COURSE CERTIFICATE

T. Harv Eker and Peak Potentials Training invite you and one family member to attend the Millionaire Mind Intensive Seminar, as complimentary guests. To register and for more information go to **www.millionairemindbook.com.**

If you have no access to a computer, call toll-free **1-888-6BeRich.***

Use Reference #_____
when you register.

(If you were not given a Reference #, use your book receipt # or special promotion code.)

---

* The offer is open to all purchasers of *Secrets of the Millionaire Mind* by T. Harv Eker. Original proof of purchase is required. The offer is limited to the Millionaire Mind Intensive weekend seminar only, and your registration in the seminar is subject to availability of space and/or changes to program schedule. This is a limited time offer and the course must be completed by the date shown on the website www.millionairemind.com. The value of this free admission for you and a companion is $2,590, as of February 2005. There will be an administration fee or deposit taken upon registration. Corporate or organizational purchasers may not use one book to invite more than two people. While participants will be responsible for their travel and other costs, admission to the program is complimentary. Participants in the seminars are under no additional financial obligation whatsoever to Peak Potentials Training or T. Harv Eker. Peak Potentials Training reserves the right to refuse admission to anyone it believes may disrupt the seminar, and to remove from the premises anyone it believes is disrupting the seminar.

SHARE THE WEALTH

The mark of true wealth is determined by
how much one can give away.
—T. Harv Eker

This book teaches you to observe your ways of thinking and to challenge your limiting, nonsupportive thoughts, habits, and actions with regard to money. The reason we start with money is that money is one of the biggest areas of pain in most people's lives. But there's a bigger picture to consider. You see, once you start recognizing your nonsupportive ways around finances, this awareness will transfer into every other part of your life.

The goal of this book has been to assist you in raising your consciousness. Again, consciousness is observing your thoughts and actions, so that you can operate from true choice in the present, rather than acting on the basis of programming from the past. It is about the power to respond from your higher self rather than to react from your fear-based, "lower" self. In this way you can be the best you can be and fulfill your destiny.

But you know what? The essence of this transformation is not just about you. It is about the entire world. Our world is nothing more than a reflection of the people who make it up. As each individual raises his or her consciousness, the world raises its consciousness—moving from fear to courage, from hatred to love, and from scarcity to prosperity for all.

It is therefore up to each of us to enlighten ourselves so that we may add more light to the world.

If you want the world to be a certain way, then start with you being that way. If you want the world to be a better place, start with *you* being better. That is why I believe it's your duty to grow yourself to your fullest potential, to create abundance and success in your life; for in doing so, you will be able to help others and add to the world in a positive way.

I therefore ask you to share this message of consciousness and empowerment with others. Get the message of this book out to as many people as possible. Commit to telling at least one hundred of your friends, family, and associates about it or consider getting it for them as a life-changing gift. Not only will they be introduced to powerful financial concepts, they will learn to observe the way they think, raise their consciousness, and in turn raise the consciousness of the planet. It would also be incredible for them to join you at the Millionaire Mind Intensive Seminar. It is truly a blessing to have your friends and family share this extraordinary experience with you. My dream is that one book, one course, one person at a time, we can change the world for the better. I ask for your support in making this dream a reality.

Thank you.

Peak Potentials Programs

Millionaire Mind Intensive Seminar—3 Days

The world-famous Millionaire Mind Intensive Seminar will transform your financial life forever. You will learn how to win the money game so that you never have to work again, as well as to reset your "money blueprint" so that financial success is natural and automatic for you.

Millionaire Mind Evening and Teleclasses

The principles of the millionaire mind are taught in evening seminars in several cities across North America as well as by teleclass. For details and schedule go to **www.millionaire mindbook.com** or call **1-888-623-7424**.

Enlightened Warrior Training Camp—4½ Days

The definition of an enlightened warrior is "one who conquers oneself." In this high-intensity program you will learn how to access your true power at will and succeed in spite of anything. By the end of this camp nothing will ever stop you again!

Wizard Training—4½ Days

Learn to manifest what you want with elegance and grace. At Wizard Training you will learn to live as the "eye of the storm," calm, centered, and peaceful in spite of anything.

Mind of Steel, Heart of Gold—6 Days

This program is the next level of both the Warrior and the Wizard. Here you will learn to dance easily and effortlessly between these two powerful energies. This camp is open only to graduates of both Enlightened Warrior and Wizard Training.

Life Directions—3 Days

The objective of this program is for you to have money with meaning. In Life Directions you will discover your true mission as well as create a vehicle that expresses this mission in a way that is highly successful in the real world. It's an absolute must for anyone wanting clarity and focus.

Train the Trainer Certification—4½ Days

Earn $20,000 a weekend teaching what you love. That's exactly what you'll learn to do at Train the Trainer. Learn everything you need to be successful in the training business, including choosing the right topic, designing an incredible program, using accelerated-learning technologies, and marketing for success. By the end of this course you will be a "hot" trainer and know exactly how to become a rich one too.

Train the Trainer II—5 Days

This program is the next level of Train the Trainer and focuses on using your full authenticity within the amazing Trainer tools that are taught. The program is open only to Train the Trainer Certification graduates.

Millionaire School—4 Days

Making your money work hard for you is one of the key elements of wealth. At Millionaire School you will learn the A–Z's of the investment world in a way that is simple and easy to understand. You'll also be introduced to investment opportunities that are usually only in the domains of the rich.

Guerrilla Business School—5 Days

At Guerrilla Business School you will learn how to create wealth quickly in any business you choose. You will learn how to create million-dollar ideas, street-smart financing, maverick marketing methods, real-world negotiation strategies, and much, much more.

Wealth and Wisdom—3 Days

Our annual extravaganza gathers many of the top authors and trainers in the world, who come together all in one place to teach how to create more money, love, and happiness in your life.

The World's Greatest Marketing Seminar—5 Days

Marketing is by far the most important skill you can own when it comes to high-speed success in business. The World's Greatest Marketing Seminar is exactly what it says, the most hands-on, experiential, effective, and intensive marketing program on the planet. In five days you will become a marketing genius. Period!

SuccessTracs Coaching—Ongoing

The best athletes in the world all have one thing in common: great coaching. SuccessTracs is a one-on-one coaching system designed to make certain you succeed in all areas of your life. The objective is simple: for you to at least double your income, double your time off, and double your speed to financial freedom. Your results will astound even you!

For full details on each of these life-changing programs, go to **www.millionairemindbook.com** or call **1-888-623-7424**.

Home Learning Programs

Many of the programs described above are available on CDs so you can learn while you drive or in the comfort of your own home.

For full details go to **www.millionairemindbook.com** or call **1-888-623-7424**.

Speaking Engagements

T. Harv Eker has been called "the most electrifying speaker on the planet." His message conveys the perfect blend of street-smart success strategies with enlightened wisdom, humor, and fun. Audiences are sky-high during his trainings, yet his lessons last a lifetime.

To have T. Harv Eker or one of our Millionaire Mind Master Trainers appear live at your next event, e-mail **speaker@peakpotentials.com** or call **1-888-623-7424**.

INDEX

Reference #: